For You

Andreas Seidl

Handover of Power

Eurpean Version

Volume 7: Labour

Imprint

Bibliographic information of the German National Library:
The German National Library lists this publication in the
German National Bibliography; detailed bibliographic data
are available on the Internet at http://dnb.dnb.de.

© 2022 Dipl. Pol. Theodor Andreas Seidl

Cover: Christiane Ebrecht
Translation: DeepL, Cologne
Production and publishing: BoD – Books on Demand,
Norderstedt

ISBN: 978-3-7568-0253-1

Acknowledgements

My thanks go to my family and friends who have made me who I am today. Special thanks to all those who supported me in writing this book. I would like to thank all my classmates, teachers, fellow students, lecturers, demonstrators, activists, colleagues, companies and countries with whom I have had the privilege of sharing the experiences from which all the ideas in this book have emerged. I would like to thank the staff of Books on Demand for their kind helpfulness. I thank the citizens of Seligenstadt for the harmony and solidarity in which I was able to write.

Foreword

This policy concept contains a variety of proposals for possible political reforms. It can be peacefully and democratically adapted to any current political system of any state in the world, but also to political systems in families, clubs, associations or companies. Wherever humans make or submit to rules that manage living together, the following proposals can be helpful. Readers who find the proposals so helpful that they would like to implement them together with like-minded people can contact the author. The contact form on the last page can be used for this purpose.

Faults and defects

I ask for your understanding that this volume was not professionally proofread. I could only afford professional proofreading for the summary. Spelling errors and unfortunate phrasing may therefore occur. As soon as this volume has sold enough to pay for a professional proofreading, it will be done. After that, a new edition will be published.

English version

Please understand that this volume has been translated automatically. I could only afford a professional translation for the summary. Poor wording and spelling errors may therefore occur. In case of doubt, the German version shall prevail. As soon as this volume has sold enough to pay for a professional translation, it will be done. After that, a new edition will be published. It was more important to me that no one in the world should have an information advantage than individual translation errors in the complete work.

References

If something has been quoted directly, it is set in italics. If the headings contain footnotes, the sources for direct and indirect quotations apply in the chapter for which the heading stands. Otherwise, quotations or source references are directly at the word or at the end of the sentence or paragraph. This book contains parts of text based on the Federal Constitution of the Swiss Confederation of 18 April 1999 (as of 12 February 2017), abbreviated to BV[1] and the Constitution of the Canton of Bern of 6 June 1993 (as of 11 March 2015), abbreviated to KV[2] .

If the constitutional paragraph, or individual paragraphs thereof, are based in whole or in part on extracts from the BV or KV, this is indicated in a footnote. The references to the corresponding footnotes for constitutional paragraphs are usually found after the heading of the affected chapter and sometimes in the body of the text. Articles used in the Swiss constitutions are listed in the footnote with a number after the title of the constitutional paragraph. Example: §123 Sample title: BV Art.123, KV Art.123.

All internet sources are fully cited in the footnotes. They were last accessed on 30.09.2021. All literature sources are also listed in full in the footnotes.

All references to tasks undertaken by other ministries and described in more detail there are given in footnotes. Example: Model Ministry - 1.2.3 Model Chapter.

All footnotes are to be viewed in comparison to the respective source, so-called indirect quotations. Direct quotations are set in italics, but hardly ever occur. The source reference is intended to enable further investigation and to take copyright

---

1 This is not an official publication. Only the publication by the Swiss Federal Chancellery is authoritative. https://www.fedlex.admin.ch/eli/cc/1999/404/de On 14.12.2021

2 This is not an official publication. The Bernese Official Collection of Laws is authoritative. https://www.belex.sites.be.ch/frontend/versions/2420?locale=de#ART71 On 16.12.2021

into account.

All keywords used, based on the names of the responsible units, departments and ministries of Germany, are listed at the end of this volume in the chapter on the conversion of ministries.

Table of contents

1 Goals of the Ministry of Labour

The objectives of the Ministry of Labour are to connect the four economic forms, to monitor the state and companies for economic efficiency and compliance with the law, and to enact laws in the field of labour law.

The goal of connecting the economic forms is achieved by ensuring freedom of movement between the economic forms through uniform access rules and regulations for companies. This will make it possible to create full employment in the country and allow the standard of living in the national economy to grow steadily in the long term.

The state and companies are regularly audited by the Company Auditing Agency and its auditors for taxation, health, economics, technology, innovation and legality. The audit results are published for citizens and consumers. They prove whether action is being taken economically, in line with costs and in accordance with the applicable laws and the constitution.

The labour laws include all the requirements of the Ministry of Labour. Their purpose is to enable citizens to exercise their control over all state activities. On the one hand, state labour law covers all conditions to which employees in the state service are entitled and obliged. On the other hand, the economic labour law covers all entrepreneurial activities, enabling citizens as independent entrepreneurs, employers and employees to see which minimum legal requirements apply to all economic forms and in which economic form more or less freedom or security is possible. All these laws make it possible for the Company Auditing Agency to audit and evaluate the work done in the country so that citizens and consumers can obtain binding results on which to base their voting behaviour.

The goal of cooperation between the ministries of labour, economy and finance is to achieve an economy that functions like a natural ecosystem that stabilises itself independently. Damage in one economic form leads to flowering in another economic form. The decisive factor here is that each blossom produces nutrients for the humans, which they can use again in other economic forms. This creates a circular economy of capital and labour, which means constant growth, like the constant build-up of biomass by the global natural ecosystem.

2 Departments

The departments are divided into sub-departments and enumerations are usually considered as their individual units. Many tasks of some departments are completely taken over by other ministries as a service.

2.1 Central Department

Part of the Central Department is the Reception Office with the Courier and Mail Room, which directs all concerns, broadcasts and visitors to the appropriate place in the ministry.

2.1.1 Staff

The Human Resources Department is responsible for staff development and planning. For this purpose, it takes care of the recruitment of junior staff, intern and trainee programmes as well as the selection procedures for employees and special selection procedures for applicants with disabilities. For politicians and employees, the department prepares a job plan. In all its tasks, it works in voting with the personnel board.[3]
All other personnel matters are transferred to the relevant ministries. The Ministry of Education is responsible for the training and further education of employees for the state service.[4] The Ministry of Infrastructure provides housing assistance for all state employees.[5] The Ministry of Finance's Pay Office takes care of staff salaries, expenses, travel and relocation costs.[6]
The Ministry of Education provides childcare for all employees

---

3 Ministry of State Organisation - 2.1.1.1 Personnel board
4 Ministry of Education - 2.1.1.1 Education and training for the state service
5 Ministry of Infrastructure - 2.1.1.1 Housing assistance for state service employees
6 Ministry of Finance - 2.1.1.1 Staff remuneration

in the state service.[7]
The Ministry of Health is responsible for the occupational health service.[8] It provides occupational health management, deals with the treatment, education and prevention of occupational accidents, controls and provides occupational health and safety through the health auditors of the Company Auditing Agency.

2.1.1.1 Service law

The Ministry of Labour handles the service law for employees in the state service. This includes labour and collective bargaining law, remuneration, personnel administration of all careers and employees, flexitime, holiday and sick leave, working time with or without flexitime in part-time or full-time at the place of employment or in home work. It regulates working conditions in the law for state enterprises, which includes ministries, agencies and state companies. The Ministry of Labour operates the Administrative Office for Personnel and Inventory for the implementation of the Service Law. The Ministry of Labour uses the Labour Directory[9] for democratic control and complaint management for citizens against state enterprises.

2.1.2 Organisation

The ministries of media, security, justice, finance, labour, state organisation provide audit services for quality management in the ministry, evaluation of work performance, revenues and expenditures, as well as prevention of corruption, protection against sabotage and, if necessary, disciplinary matters.[10]
The language service for translating talks or texts is provided by the Ministry of Education.[11] The Ministry of Finance organises

---

7 Ministry of Education - 2.1.1.2 Childcare for state service employees
8 Ministry of Health - 2.1.1.1 Occupational Health Service
9 Ministry of Digital - 12 Directories
10 Ministries of Media, Security, Justice, Finance, State Organisation - 2.1.2.1 Audit services
11 Ministry of Education - 2.1.3 Language Service

the annual budget vote and ensures proper accounting in each ministry.[12] It regulates budget procedures, budget law, staff budgets, departmental budgets, costs and cash management, and assists ministries in budget planning for the budget vote. The Ministry of Digital Affairs supports the supply of Information Technology.[13] In voting with the Procurement Office of the Ministry of Labour, it takes care of the procurement, provision, maintenance and service of technical devices and software. Much of this is produced in-house to ensure data protection in information and communication technology. Information technology and digitalisation officers audit and advise the ministries. Digital appointment calendar and documentation services are provided as well as a digital policy archive including a library.

2.1.2.1 Audit services

The auditors of the Company Auditing Agency for Business, Innovation, Technology and Health ensure appropriate quality management in companies and state enterprises as well as ongoing evaluation of key economic figures, continuous improvement of products and operating procedures, safety of technical equipment and products and compliance with laws on occupational safety and environmental protection. To prevent corruption, the tax auditors check the flow of funds. For sabotage protection, the innovation auditors examine product piracy. For sabotage protection, the legality auditors investigate individual suspected employees to see if they are preparing criminal offences in the course of their work. The legality auditors ensure the investigation and enforcement of disciplinary matters.

---

12 Ministry of Finance - 8 state revenues, 9 state expenditure
13 Ministry of Digital Affairs - 2.1.2.1.1 Supply of Information Technology

2.1.2.2 State procurement

State procurement is handled by the Procurement Office of the Ministry of Labour. All ministries turn to the Procurement Office for the award of state contracts and place their orders there. The Ministry of Labour regulates procurement law by issuing requirements to the Procurement Office.

2.2 Management Department

The Management Department is the minister's department. With his office team, he provides policy planning and analysis for his ministry and coordinates the relationship between the nation and the municipality through exchanges with his deputies in the municipalities. He initiates cooperation with other ministries or citizens in committees and is supported by the Ministry of State Organisation.

The Ministry of Media Affairs, through its media service, provides press and public relations for the ministry, moderates civil dialogue, trains or provides a spokesperson for the minister, writes speeches and texts on request, and ensures the implementation of conferences and events.[14]

The Ministry of Digital Affairs is responsible for digital management and thus provides departmental management. It automatically produces business statistics, staff surveys and the current state of research through statistics. It automatically forwards proposals to the affected or empowered state employees. In document management, it ensures digitalisation and that ministries share forms with each other.[15]

2.3 European Department

The Ministry of Foreign Affairs ensures the constant transmission of the latest information on current European policy affecting the respective ministry, applicable European Union law and all European Union funding programmes

---

14 Ministry of Media Affairs - 2.2.1.1 Media Service
15 Ministry of Digital Affairs - 2.1.2.1 Digital Service

starting or in progress.[16] The European Department, in cooperation with the Ministry of Foreign Affairs, oversees the making of law and implementation of European labour policy in the European Union internal market.

The European Department decides for the areas of employment and social policy[17] , agriculture[18] , fisheries , consumer protection[19][20] , consumer - general provisions[21] , competition[22] and companies[23] whether to adopt, adapt or reject existing European Union law.[24]

2.4 Labour Department

The Labour Department, in cooperation with all other ministries, ensures the existence of state enterprises and information on applicable labour laws in state enterprises. It ensures and supervises the operation of the administration and procurement offices.

In cooperation with the Ministry of Education, the Labour Department ensures the implementation of the requirements in vocational education and training. In cooperation with the Ministry of Foreign Affairs, it ensures the domestic implementation of European and international labour policy. After consultation with the Minister of Labour, further draft legislation on European and international labour policy is prepared.

The Labour Department operates the Labour Directory in cooperation with the Ministry of Digital Affairs and oversees its operation. It receives suggestions and problems that citizens

16 Ministry of Foreign Affairs - 2.4 European Department

17 https://eur-lex.europa.eu/summary/chapter/employment_and_social_policy.html?root_default=SUM_1_CODED=17

18 https://eur-lex.europa.eu/summary/chapter/agriculture.html?root_default=SUM_1_CODED=03

19 https://eur-lex.europa.eu/summary/chapter/0206.html

20 https://eur-lex.europa.eu/summary/chapter/0904.html

21 https://eur-lex.europa.eu/summary/chapter/0901.html

22 https://eur-lex.europa.eu/summary/chapter/competition.html?root_default=SUM_1_CODED=08

23 https://eur-lex.europa.eu/summary/chapter/enterprise.html?root_default=SUM_1_CODED=19

24 Ministry of Foreign Affairs - 6.4 Conversion of political contents to the policy of dynamic media democracy

and state workers have in handling the Labour Directory. If the Ministry of Labour is able to find a solution, the Labour Department will do so. It forwards technical problems and suggestions to the digital service.[25]

The Labour Department ensures the operation of the Employment Office and coordinates its cooperation with the ministries for the economy. It ensures the proper calculation of compensation payments between economic forms.

The Labour Department oversees the retirement models of the ministries of economy and, in consultation with the Minister of Economy, ensures that retirement age legislation is drafted.

2.5 Company Department

The Company Department, in cooperation with the ministries of economy, ensures compliance with the principles of hybrid economies and resolves conflicts over responsibilities and distributions between the ministries of economy. It ensures the realisation of free movement between economic forms through the operation of Citizens' Insurance.

The Company Department oversees the implementation of enterprise policy requirements by the ministries of economy and informs them of innovations. It involves all ministries of economy and the Minister of Labour in drafting legislation. It oversees compliance with the requirements for the protection of employees and consumers through appropriate measures in the ministries of economy. In cooperation with the ministries of economics and finance, it enforces the requirements for the finance economy. In cooperation with the Ministries of Economic Affairs and Health, it enforces the requirements for agriculture. The Company Department oversees the Food Directory and operates it in cooperation with the Ministry of Digital Affairs.

---

25 Ministry of Digital Affairs - 2.1.2.1 Digital Service

2.6 Audit Department

The Audit Department ensures the operation of the Company Auditing Agency in cooperation with the Ministries of Finance, Economy, Health, Innovation, Security, Justice and Education. It oversees the operation of the audit services of the Ministry of Labour, namely the Company Auditing Agency, the Antitrust Agency and the Financial Supervisory Authority. The Audit Department oversees and operates the Consumer Directory and the Success Model Directory in cooperation with the Ministry of Digital Affairs. In cooperation with the Ministry of Education, the Audit Department ensures the operation of the Institute for Evaluation.

3 Tasks of the Ministry of Labour

The Ministry of Labour's task is to manage the state economy efficiently. The task is fulfilled by administering state enterprises according to uniform procedures, procuring funds centrally and paying personnel according to tariff and performance. The Ministry of Economy is responsible for labour legislation that affects all economic forms, regulates the switching of goods and persons between economic forms, ensures smooth cooperation between ministries of economy and leads to sustained full employment.

The Ministry of Labour's task is to enable the coexistence of four economic forms and the free movement of citizens between them. The task is fulfilled by a circular economy that provides balance and support between the economic forms and enables full employment. Free movement is ensured by regulating the movement of humans and things. Citizens' Insurance is used to bring insurance services and the switching tax is used to change assets. The end of free movement is regulated for foreigners, goods and services in foreign trade regulations. For domestic citizens, freedom of movement ends when they retire. The Ministry of Labour's task is to provide a secure pension. This task is fulfilled by the pension models of the ministries of economy and a flexible retirement age.

The Ministry of Labour pursues a labour policy that provides sufficient opportunities for work. This task is fulfilled by promoting the labour market in such a way that persons can fulfil their career aspirations. This is ensured by agreements on vocational training with the Ministries of Education, Innovation and Economic Affairs and on European and international labour policy with the Ministry of Foreign Affairs. The Employment Office is responsible for passive and active labour market promotion. The Labour Directory is primarily used to place the labour market under as much competition as possible. Companies are also given the opportunity to map the market for goods and services in the Labour Directory by offering their products there. In this way, the Labour Directory makes it possible for all suppliers in the country to face all demanders in the country.

The Ministry of Labour's enterprise policy concerns all companies of all economic forms equally. In this way, the Ministry of Labour can fulfil the task of creating equal opportunities for all companies without harming humans and nature. The task is considered fulfilled when the environment, entrepreneurs, employees and consumers are sufficiently protected and dominant monopolies that lead to the redistribution of assets to individuals are broken up or excluded.

Special requirements are issued by the Ministry of Labour in voting with the Ministry of Finance for the finance economy. This regulates joint-stock companies, gambling and stock exchange trading and is supervised by the Financial Supervisory Authority. For agriculture, the Ministry of Labour, in voting with the Ministries of Economy and Health, issues specific requirements and measures for conversion to permaculture and agribusiness. This task is considered fulfilled as soon as the prices per kilogram for most foodstuffs are approximately the same and even healthy food accounts for a maximum of 10% of the cost of living.

The Ministry of Labour's task is to regularly inspect all state enterprises and private companies for compliance with requirements and worker satisfaction in order to operate a stable, growing national economy. This task is fulfilled by the Company Auditing Agency with the auditors for taxation, health, economics, technology, innovation and legality, as well as the business consultants. The Company Auditing Agency's task is to ensure that all companies can make profits in the long term if possible and still comply with all the laws of their economic form.

4 State enterprises[26]

State enterprises are workplaces of ministries, namely offices, agencies, companies and enterprises established by ministries. The Ministry of Labour is responsible for the overall human resources management of all state service employees, leaving only the recruitment of new staff and their performance evaluation partly within the remit of individual ministries.

The Ministry of Labour sets the labour law that governs careers, collective bargaining, working hours, place of employment, pay and expense allowances for all state employees.

All state enterprises established on behalf of the people provide services with which they may earn a maximum of 10% profit above cost recovery. State enterprises are established and administered by the ministries. The Ministry of Labour is responsible for ensuring business efficiency in all state enterprises and audits all state enterprises through the Social Market Economy and Innovation Auditors of the Company Auditing Agency.

Companies working on behalf of the state must be registered in either the Planned Economy or Social Market Economy. When it comes to orders such as the production of patents, weapons or computer parts for People's Computers and voting computers, special secrecy and loyalty apply. These orders may only be awarded to Planned Enterprise .[27]

4.1 Foundation

Whether state enterprises are to be established, privatised or closed down is decided by affected citizens and politicians. As soon as municipal or national laws are enacted that include a service, it must be clarified whether the state should provide

26§199 State enterprises
27Ministry of Planned Economy - 10.5 Planned Enterprise

the service through a state enterprise or whether companies in the market economies should be founded or commissioned to provide the service. This excludes services provided by the ministries of security, justice and digital affairs.

4.2 Natural monopolies

Most natural monopolies are state enterprises, at least initially. Natural monopolies are characterised by having very high initial investments, but then vanishingly low costs for supporting another customer. Examples are the postal service, railways, sewage and energy industries. The initiative for this can come from politicians or People's Innovation Company. Since natural monopolies cost a lot of money before they can generate a lot of money, any natural monopolies must be wanted by a majority of the population and be approved accordingly in the budget vote.

4.3 Construction and maintenance

State enterprises are built, equipped and maintained by the Construction Team of the Ministry of Infrastructure.[28] Together with the future employees, the responsible politicians and affected citizens, the Construction Team's architectural office plans the building project. At the end of the planning process, the construction project is presented virtually in a committee[29] and publicly negotiated in a show on Government Television.[30] Afterwards, changes are only possible if a newly convened committee is held.

Funds for construction and equipment come either from the state budget, if these costs were approved in the budget vote, or from corporate bonds on the People's Stock Exchange[31]. In this case, the 70% of the profits are used to pay back the bonds with interest. Once all the debts have been paid off, the 70% of the profits go into the state budget.

---

28 Ministry of Infrastructure - 5.8 Construction Team
29 Ministry of State Organisation - 9.6 Committee
30 Ministry of Media Affairs - 5.7.1 On the spot, 7.2.3.5 Solution Finder
31 Ministry of Finance - 11.8 People's Stock Exchange

4.4 Entrepreneurial action of the state

All operations in the ministries and their state enterprises are made possible through the use of money and property by employees. The Ministry of Labour, through the Company Auditing Agency, monitors the operations and use of money, assets and staff. In doing so, ministries are obliged to use personnel and capital in such a way that there is no wasteful excess or persistent shortage, but rather consistent state budget surpluses of between 5 and 10 per cent and slow and steady growth in living standards through technical and moral progress.

4.5 Publication obligation

All state enterprises must disclose all their activities in the State Directory. They publish their digital administration, which makes all prices paid and services rendered visible. This does not include names of service recipients, which are subject to data protection. Employees and business partners are named for all costs they incur. This data serves as an accountability report for the budget vote.

4.6 Profits[32]

All state enterprises of all ministries are allowed to make a combined profit of up to 10%. If profits are higher, these amounts must be transferred to the state budget for the following year. A ministry can ask in the budget vote to be allowed to save the surplus amounts in order to implement reforms. In the absence of a savings plan, state enterprises must reduce their prices until a total of 10% is reached. The fees for a service may be increased by 10% in addition to the cost recovery price. 30% of the profits are distributed to the employees as bonuses. 70% of the profits are booked to the ministry's account at the People's Bank[33] , to which a state enterprise belongs. In the budget vote, the citizens can then

32§154 Tax reduction
33Ministry of Finance - 11 People's Bank

distribute this money among the ministries like all the other tax money. Exceptions are made for People's Innovation Companies, which have no profit ceiling when exporting abroad and always try to make monopoly profits.

The aim is to use the profits to reward employees based on performance, to keep the ministry and its state enterprises modern and to be able to reduce taxes. In the first step, business tax will be used less and less to finance the state, but will be paid out to the citizens via the Unconditional Basic Income[34] . Only when state financing is handled exclusively through value added tax can value added tax be reduced in the second step.

4.7 Direct democratic work organisation

The work instructions come from the responsible ministry, which is led by elected politicians. How these work instructions are completed with the least amount of manpower and materials is the responsibility of the employees. The Company Auditing Agency records efficient working practices and can declare them binding for all state enterprises that fulfil the same services.

In state enterprises, there is a heterarchically organised direct democratic mode of operation. All leaders, except politicians, can be degraded by a vote of no confidence by their subordinates and a new election called. All non-elected leadership positions must be filled by rotation.[35]

Teams elect their own team leaders, organise duty rosters collectively and vote on who can do what and how much. All colleagues who are affected by a superior elect their superior directly through an election of persons process or by rotation. Superiors can be replaced after a set period of time or up to a set percentage through a quorum. The rotation procedure specifies who is next in line.

As is usual in heterarchical procedures, all workers are sorted according to qualifications and activities, but they have equal rights and work independently in their area of responsibility.

34 Ministry of Finance - 6 Unconditional Basic Income
35 Ministry of State Organisation - 8.4.3 Internal heterarchy

If problems arise, they are first solved jointly by all affected colleagues. If this is not possible, all colleagues participate in the solution finding process and jointly vote on the solution to be adopted and who is responsible for its implementation and monitoring, usually for a limited period of time.

4.8 Labour law for employees in state enterprises

The Ministry of Labour regulates the labour law for employees in state enterprises in the So-called state service law. Employees in state enterprises are subject to the same labour law and insurance benefits as employees of the Social Market Economy.[36] Employees in state enterprises may only be nationals. Every employee has the right to work part-time, flexitime or full-time at the place of work or at home, provided that all the services required by law can be provided. The conciliation board of the Ministry of Labour shall, if necessary, review and enforce the agreement.

4.8.1 Collective bargaining

Collective bargaining is conducted by the ministers of the responsible ministries and the ministers of labour and finance on the employers' side. There is a separate state service labour union for employees in state enterprises. Collective bargaining[37] negotiates collective labour agreements for the different occupational groups in the state service, which include minimum requirements for the respective labour contract[38]. Collective bargaining takes place before the annual budget vote[39], where the people can decide on wage levels and whether to retain or eliminate a position. State employees are either members of the branch union for all state employees or are included in the branch union that their ministry has specified for their job, in voting with their employees.

---

36 Ministry of Social Market Economy - 7 Employee protection, 17.5 Compulsory insurance
37 Ministry of Social Market Economy - 8.4 Collective bargaining
38 Ministry of Social Market Economy - 9 Employment contract
39 Ministry of Finance - 9.5 Budget vote

4.8.2 Bonus-malus system

The binding wages paid are set in the collective labour agreements. In addition, state enterprises can pay bonuses to their employees, which amount to a maximum of 30% of profits. Who receives what share of the profits as a bonus in addition to the monthly salary is determined in the annual performance evaluations. Bonuses are paid with the last monthly salary of the year.

A bonus will only be paid if performance recipients and auditors of the Company Auditing Agency identify a particular performance of a specific employee or team in an interview or audit. Benefit recipients may be superiors, other departments or customers who are interviewed as part of the Company Auditing Agency's annual audit. Company Auditing Agency auditors use business figures and surveys to review each employee's performance. Three indicators determine the amount of bonuses paid. They are multiplied together and the result is multiplied by an employee's annual salary and treaty bonus to calculate an employee's bonus.

4.8.2.1 Ministry indicator

The ministry indicator shows how much profit the ministry has made overall and how much the bonus fund is filled. For example, if some businesses have made losses and others profits, less or no bonus is paid out. The business indicator can range between 0% and 1.3% and is multiplied by the payable bonus amount.

4.8.2.2 Performance indicator

The performance indicator includes the speed of work, punctuality, completeness and harmlessness displayed in the delivery of the service by the employee in the past year. The integrity is also covertly audited and certified in the Company Auditing Agency's annual audit. Employees must adhere to these certified procedures and also check their own performance.

For the question: "Was the service provided quickly, on time, completely and without hesitation?" a mark between 0.5 and 1.5 can be given for each adjective in the question. The question is also included in the questionnaire that employees and their superiors must complete as part of the audit. The marks have the following meaning: 0.5 means "poor", 1 means "good" and 1.5 means "better".

The performance indicator is calculated by taking the average of the auditor and staff ratings, adding them together and dividing the result by four.

4.8.2.3 Behaviour indicator

The employees receive information about their work attitude with the behaviour indicator and another factor to calculate their bonus. For all characteristics, scores between 0.5 and 1.5 can be given by those who are asked the corresponding questions. The scores have the following meaning: 0.5 means "bad", 1 means "good" and 1.5 means "better".

4.8.2.3.1 Quality

Has the employee improved the quality of the service?
This question is asked to the employee, his/her superior and beneficiary. In the case of employee statements, examples of quality improvement must be listed. For example, a sustainable solution could have been found on how to detect faults and methods on how to prevent these faults from occurring in the future.

4.8.2.3.2 Top performance

Did the employee perform better than was required of him/her?
This question is asked of the employee and his/her direct superior. Overtime worked is automatically listed here as well as the work rate in output per hour. For example, projects that were initiated independently or work assignments that were

fully completed before the weekend through overtime can be indicated.

4.8.2.3.3 Cooperation

Did the employee support the team?
This question is asked of the employee and all employees who work with him or her on a daily basis, as well as the direct superior. Improvements in business figures attributable to this worker are automatically listed here, entered in the Labour Directory as part of the audit for the worker's area of accountability. For example, long queues may have been worked through, allowing turnover to increase more quickly.

4.8.2.3.4 Innovation

Did the employee bring in an improvement that made the service or service delivery the same or better with less effort?
This question is asked of the employee and his/her superiors who are responsible for the implementation of improvement proposals. If the proposal has already been entered in the Ideas Directory[40] , these entries are automatically listed here with their heading and entry number. For example, new technology for service delivery may have been introduced or developed in-house.

4.8.2.3.5 Integrity

Was the employee reliable, honest, loyal and peaceful?
This question is asked of every direct superior and employee who has worked with the affected employee. The authors are anonymised and only the result is given to the affected employee. Here, each adjective of the question can be given a mark between 1 and 3.

---

40 Ministry of Innovation - 8 Ideas Directory

4.8.2.4 Example calculation

0.5 = poor - someone has performed below average - 50%.
1 = good - someone has shown average performance - 100%.
1.5 = better - someone has shown above-average performance - 150%.

Performance indicator	Company Auditing Agency auditor	Employees	Superior	Average
Working speed	0,5	1	0,7	0,73
Punctuality	1	1	1	1
Completeness	0,6	0,8	0,8	0,73
Harmlessness	1	1	0,9	0,96
Final grade				0,86

Behaviour indicator	Company Auditing Agency auditor	Employees	Team	Superior	Customers	Average
Quality		1		1	1,1	1,03
Top performance	0,8	0,6		0,7		0,7
Cooperation	1,2	1,5	1,5	1,4		1,4
Innovation	1	1		1		1
Integrity			1,5	1,5		1,5
Final grade						1,13

The results of the Company Auditing Agency auditor come from the automatic messages from the Labour Directory and Ideas Directory.

Ministry indicator
The ministry made 5% profits last year, so only half as much in bonuses can be paid out. The indicator is 50%, i.e. 0.5.

Final account
Annual salary in € * contractual bonus in % * performance

indicator * behaviour indicator * ministry indicator = bonus payment for current year

Example: 30 000€ * 0,1 * 0,86 * 1,13 * 0,5 = 1457,70€

5 Administrative Office

The Administrative Office is responsible for the administration of all ministries, state enterprises and state service employees. It performs all the tasks provided for in the labour law for state employees.

5.1 Digital personnel management

Times for work, overtime, leave and sickness are recorded and administered via the Labour Directory. If an action is required by a worker, he or she automatically receives a message from the Labour Directory about what needs to be done. If the task is completed, a message is automatically sent to the superior. If it is not completed within the specified period, the message is also sent to the Administrative Office. If tasks are not completed even after personal consultation, a warning will be issued and, if necessary, termination. Changes in the duty roster and conversion to part-time, full-time, flexitime or home-based work are coordinated with the responsible workers via the Labour Directory. If there are distribution disputes and dissatisfaction, the arbitration board can be called in. It then automatically receives access rights to view and edit the history of duty rosters and time recording.

5.2 Conciliation board

The conciliation board is responsible for all employee concerns. It can examine motions for part-time, flexitime, full-time or home-based work for feasibility and approve or reject them. Rejection must be on the grounds of impracticability. Approval obliges affected state enterprises to implement and, where appropriate, rotate employees through periods of home-based or part-time work. If requests accumulate at the conciliation board, it may convene a staff committee to negotiate disagreements in labour law and develop solutions. The current committee procedure for laws is used, with all those affected employees entitled to vote.

5.3 Cost centre

The cost centre is responsible for settling costs for wages, official travel, moves, assistance measures for impaired employees and equipment with materials, furniture and intact buildings. State enterprises submit the costs for the Construction Team of the Ministry of Infrastructure to the cost centre. Materials and furniture are ordered through the Procurement Office.

The cost centre works with the Ministry of Finance and participates in the annual budget vote in which it solicits its funds for the coming year.

5.4 Occupational Safety and Health Officer

The Company Auditing Agency's health auditors are responsible for audits and advice on occupational safety and health measures. In occupational safety and health, the Ministry of Labour is advised by the Institute of Occupational Health[41] to ensure safe working conditions in all state enterprises. The Company Auditing Agency verifies compliance with occupational health and safety regulations in its annual audit of all state enterprises.

6 Procurement Office

The Procurement Office procures the necessary means of production, goods and services for all ministries and their state enterprises. In voting with the Minister of Labour, the procurement law is formulated and submitted to the people for a vote. Goods and services are purchased from domestic companies. Foreign suppliers may only be used if the product is not available from a domestic company. The Procurement Office acts similar to a Planned Economy Buyers

41 Ministry of Health - 4.5.5 Institute of Occupational Health

Association[42] . All responsible politicians and state employees, are the customers. All customers report their wishes and how quickly they need the goods or services. The Procurement Office ensures that as many customers as possible agree on the same product in order to be able to negotiate quantity discounts. When selecting products, attention is paid to life-cycle oriented procurement. This means requiring durable products, environmentally friendly production methods and fair working conditions, from the extraction of raw materials through production and consumption to disposal and recycling.

6.1 Logistics

The Procurement Office has its own logistics department, which cooperates with the Social Service's driving department. If other domestic logistics companies offer the same service to the Social Market Economy at a cheaper price, these companies become logistics service providers for the Procurement Office.

6.2 Catalogue

The catalogue is updated annually, all products below 10% order frequency are removed from the catalogue. On the Procurement Office intranet site, users have the option of posting a desired item to be included in the range. The article is added to a wish list where it can be rated by other users.[43] Popular items are added to the catalogue. Citizens can also order items from the catalogue and thereby increase sales.

7 People's Innovation Company

People's Innovation Companies are special state enterprises run by the Ministry of Innovation and audited, monitored and advised by the Ministry of Labour through the Company Auditing Agency. They produce innovations and make most of their monopoly profits available to the state treasury. They

42 Ministry of Planned Economy - 9.4.4.2 Buyer Associations
43 Ministry of Planned Economy - 9.4.4.2 Buyer Associations

are closed down as soon as they make losses exceeding the last annual profit for 2 consecutive years. They are privatised[44] as soon as they can no longer generate monopoly profits.

8 Theory of hybrid economic systems

In the past, there was already a barter economy, planned economy, social market economy and free market economy. What is new is the simultaneous practice of all four economic forms of the past in one country. The citizens have the election between a nature-based way of life, as in primeval times, a communal way of life, as in communism, a social way of life, as in socialism, and a free way of life, as in capitalism. In contrast to the dictatorial political systems in which communism, socialism and capitalism existed, the dynamic media democracy still applies here. For programmes and voting, scientific theories are used on the basis of which communism, socialism and capitalism were once developed and adapted to the present time and democratic circumstances. Faults of the past are avoided by the ministries for media and digital affairs informing the citizens about the ways of life in the states with communism, socialism and capitalism and involving them directly democratically in today's implementation.

9 Principles of hybrid economies[45]

The four economic forms are the Barter Economy, Planned Economy, Social Market Economy and Free Market Economy. They function as four different economic systems in one country. There is a ministry for each economic form and all ministries of economy are harmonised by the Ministry of Labour. This enables citizens to make their own personal decision on the weighting of state-granted freedom and security in their lives. According to the theories of dynamic media democracy[46] , citizens should be able to make decisions that affect only their personal lives. Decisions that affect the

44Ministry of Innovation - 10.6 Privatisation
45§46,4 State, §210,1,2 Principles of economic order   : BV Art. 94, KV Art.50
46Ministry of State Organisation - 5 Theories of Dynamic Media Democracy

lives of other humans must be voted on with the other humans. The more citizens are affected by a decision, the greater the number of those entitled to vote. There are four economic ministers. One each for Barter Economy, Planned Economy, Social Market Economy, Free Market Economy. This allows citizens to elect the leader of an economic form individually and deselect them in case of mismanagement.

The citizens decide through their consumption and their labour in which economic form they participate. They do this by earning the respective currency through gainful employment and spending it through consumption. It is possible for persons to own several companies in different economic forms. Through their place of residence, citizens decide whether they have bought or rented housing in a Barter Economy Zone[47] , a Social Village or in the rest of the country in the Social Market Economy or Free Market Economy.

9.1 Freedom and security

Freedom and security are mutually restrictive. The four economic forms are intended to resolve the conflict between freedom and security in economic policy. The four economic forms divide freedom and security as well as poverty and wealth. The Ministry of Barter Economy offers conditions in which citizens can be free and poor. The Ministry of Planned Economy offers conditions in which citizens can be safe and poor. The Ministry of Social Market Economy provides conditions in which citizens can be safe and rich. The Ministry of Free Market Economy provides conditions in which citizens can be free and rich. The state provides services in the Planned Economy and the Social Market Economy that make life safer and the poor richer.

---

47 Ministry of Barter Economy - 6 Barter Economy Zone

9.2 Property[48]

Property can be acquired through purchase, exchange, donation or own production. Taking possession of things from the environment is only possible for things that do not belong to anyone else. Humans can only declare themselves the property of another human and for this they need a written treaty, which must be certified by the Registry Office by mutual agreement.[49] Ownership entitles the owner to determine the use to which it is put. It obliges the owner to dispose of it properly after its use, so that the environment and third parties do not suffer any disadvantages. Property that can be picked up for disposal must be marked as such. It can then be appropriated by passers-by before the disposal company takes possession of it. Further use is encouraged within the framework of the circular economy.[50]

9.3 Laws and taxes for companies[51]

Depending on which Ministry of Economy a company is under, it must comply with the laws and pay taxes there. Business taxes are usually different in each economic form. The amount of taxes necessary to manage an economic form is determined by the respective Ministry of Economy, which submits the proposal for the coming year during the annual budget vote.

9.4 Circuit of economic forms

The economic forms complement and stabilise each other. The Barter Economy serves the citizens to decelerate, be down-to-earth and close to nature. In it, they can support themselves through work and do not need any money. The Barter Economy is specialised in surviving without modern technology. The Planned Economy serves the citizens to

---

48§25,1,3 Property guarantee: BV Art.26
49Ministry of Family Affairs - 6 Registry Office
50Ministry of Health - 6.7.2.1 Circular economy
51§228.1 Labour: BV Art. 110

further their human capital and maximise their leisure time. In it, they support themselves through compulsory work and can try out business ideas. The Planned Economy specialises in recycling surplus and waste from the market economies. The Social Market Economy serves the citizens to support each other in solidarity, to protect their environment and to secure their standard of living. In it, they can accumulate wealth that they can hardly lose again. The Social Market Economy specialises in providing insurance and cooperatives. The Free Market Economy serves citizens to participate in international competition. In it, they can take high risks that can make individuals very successful or fail miserably. The Free Market Economy specialises in interfering as little as possible with economic freedom.

As a circuit, a citizen can, for example, fail in the Free Market Economy with high debts, file for personal bankruptcy, wait in the Barter Economy for the deadline to save money again, get another educational qualification in the Planned Economy, find business partners and start a company. This company can grow up in the Social Market Economy until it reaches a size that can survive in the world market and moves to the Free Market Economy. For example, the circuit of a product can start as an outdated broken computer in the Free Market Economy, which is repaired in the Planned Economy, used and sold to the Social Market Economy, where it is then modernised, sold to the Social Market Economy and offered on the world market.

9.5 Structural support[52]

The Ministry of Labour ensures that state enterprises and zones of Barter Economy and Planned Economy are located in parts of the country that are supported by poor public infrastructure and few jobs. When industries and suppliers face economic hardship despite demand, the Ministry of Labour, through ministries and economic forms, can temporarily support the industry and suppliers with free or credit-financed offers. These offers consist of either advice from the Company Auditing

<hr>

52 §212,1-3,6 Structural policy: BV Art. 103

Agency's business consultants or the granting of a loan by the People's Bank. The support lasts only until a higher price could be achieved or losses could be avoided and profits or a cost-covering business could be built up. The loans have to be repaid as soon as the company starts making profits again. The repayment rates are added to the company's business tax. The rates are 60% of the profits before tax deduction. The economic auditors check the creditworthiness and the repayment. If money is not the best solution, business advice from the Company Auditing Agency's business consultants is provided by the Ministry of Labour. The costs must be reimbursed as soon as the advisors' measures are successful. The repayment rates are the same as for a loan.

9.6 Revitalisation and decommissioning of economic systems[53]

When there is strong demand in an economic form for its products and jobs, the economic system is invigorated. The number of users increases and capacities are expanded. The increasing turnover leads to increasing revenues for the affected Ministry of Economy. Of these additional revenues, a share determined by the Ministry of Labour goes to the Ministry of Economy whose economic form suffers the most from the growth of the other economic form. If several economic forms are affected, the share is distributed among them according to the contraction. The remaining part of the additional revenues from growth is used to expand capacity for the increasing number of users.

When there is weak demand in an economic form for its products and jobs, the economic system is shut down. If the number of users decreases, capacities are reduced, if they are intended for this purpose. Capacities are shut down if they are suitable to be reactivated when the economic system is revived. The complete disappearance of an economic form is prevented by the Ministry of Labour. An economic form that is not in demand must at least be preserved as a museum. Citizens have the right to live in this museum at any time as

53 §161,1-3 Financial and burden equalisation: BV Art. 135

long as they follow the rules of this economic form. These pioneers have the right to revive the economic form with the help of the museum's equipment.

9.7 Balancing between the economic forms[54]

Each economic form should be able to exist independently. As soon as economic forms influence each other, the Ministry of Labour intervenes and ensures that finances and burdens are balanced. As soon as the existence of an economic form is threatened, the other economic forms support the threatened economic form through compensation payments. At least once a year, before the budget vote, a committee must decide on equalisation payments. Compensation payments are justified if geographical, topographical or socio-demographic conditions overreach or disadvantage an economic form. Favoured economic forms support disadvantaged economic forms. Advice is given in committees on how the disadvantages could be resolved so that compensatory payments are not a permanent solution.

The tax burden should be distributed in all economic forms in such a way that 110% of the costs of tax-funded state services are covered. In order to keep up with international tax competition, the Free Market Economy can do without state services and regularisation for its companies.

9.8 Full employment

Through the four economic forms, the state can enable its nationals to find gainful employment in at least one economic form that enables them to earn a living. The Employment Office ensures that there is always full employment and that nationals can easily switch between economic forms. All nationals who cannot find work in the Barter Economy, Social Market Economy and Free Market Economy can live in the Planned Economy. They are free to remain there or to start a company or find employment in another economic

---

54§161,1-3 Financial and burden equalisation: BV Art. 135

form to support themselves. Foreigners must take out private insurance against unemployment. The Labour Directory digitally displays the supply and demand of workers and uses an algorithm to connect them with suitable partners. The Employment Office also offers other employment exchange services.

The central concern is that all nationals should be as free as possible to choose the economic form in which they wish to work. So there may be nationals who necessarily live in the Social Village but would actually prefer to live in the Social Market Economy or Free Market Economy. They are the So-called unemployed. Job seekers can be unemployed and working people. For nationals and naturalised unemployed foreigners, the Employment Office provides active labour market support. The Employment Office provides measures for employment exchange and operates the Labour Directory to facilitate vocational retraining and to promote reintegration into the desired economic form. For nationals, this can happen while living in the Social Village.

Full employment raises wages, which is desirable in order to strengthen purchasing power. However, with a slight delay, prices also rise, which only leads to a devaluation of money instead of an increase in living standards and should therefore be avoided. The Central Bank can manage the key interest rate for the individual currencies in order to have the money earn interest at the rate of inflation. The Ministry of Labour tries to avoid Central Bank intervention by allowing rising unit labour costs to be offset by rising productivity and automation. If the same amount can be produced with less labour, the prices of goods and services can remain the same, but wages rise. Increasing productivity is ensured by the innovation auditors of the Company Auditing Agency. This happens, among other things, through the possibility for employees and entrepreneurs to make suggestions for improvements and to market them via the innovation auditors.

9.9 Deadlines

In the short term, free world trade will only be possible in the Free Market Economy. As long as anarchy prevails internationally and money knows no borders, but persons and certain goods do, other national economic forms must be withdrawn from this location competition. Behind location competition is a process of exploitation through a lower standard of living in another country with a weak currency and lower labour rights. This exploitation leads to many poor people becoming poorer and a few rich people becoming richer. This global redistribution and expropriation can only be escaped by shielding companies and markets in their own stock exchanges, production sites, sales areas and currencies.

In the medium term, the laws and the standard of living between states are aligned in such a way that the Social Market Economy can offer its rules, goods and services on the common market in all participating states. As soon as states also establish a Barter Economy or Planned Economy with the same standards, persons and goods can also move freely here.

In the long term, the rules for the four economic forms apply worldwide. However, municipal exceptions can be agreed in accordance with the constitution.

9.10 Division of humans and space

Every economic form needs space and humans to develop. Therefore, the number of persons and nationals living and working inland who are currently in the various economic forms is continuously recorded. In particular, the two limited zones of Planned Economy and Barter Economy should be able to grow when more nationals want to move in and shrink when fewer nationals live there. In the rest of the country, building land must be expelled.

Therefore, the developed, undeveloped, inhabited, uninhabited and cultivated land is recorded in square metres. It is recorded with what it is overgrown or cultivated with and at what height it is located. Airspace is recorded in cubic metres, temperatures and wind strength per metre of height. The lake area is recorded in cubic metres, temperatures per metre depth, tidal range and inflow and outflow velocities at river mouths. At river mouths, the amount of water in cubic metres that flows through per second is also measured. The river area is recorded in cubic metres per day, temperatures per metre depth, estuary volume per second and river velocity. The sea area is recorded in cubic metres, temperatures per metre depth, tidal range per square metre in metres and wave height. The data is collected via satellite. The data is fed into the Labour Directory and can be accessed in the computer game "Policy Manager"[55] and the Algoracle .[56]

The population statistics are also included in the overall calculation. The number of humans living in cities and in rural areas, the age structure and other statistically anonymised data from the directories[57] .

The value of the population is measured by human capital, which consists of health (Health Directory), training (Education Directory), work experience (Labour Directory), birth rate, suicide rate, divorce rate and life expectancy (Persons Directory). To make happiness measurable, citizens can be asked directly through referendums what makes them happy and how much of it they have. The response options are: "too little, just right, too much". The ideal situation is a stable population with an average of 2.1 children per woman and a high number of high educational qualifications.

The assets in the country in cash and in kind are calculated through tax rates, data from the Real Estate Directory[58] , Labour Directory and the audit reports of the Company Auditing Agency. Ongoing costs to maintain the assets are documented and put into a reasonable price-performance ratio.

---

55 Ministry of Digital Affairs - 15.5 Policy Manager
56 Ministry of Digital Affairs - 15.3 Algoracle
57 Ministry of Digital Affairs - 12.9 Directory Register
58 Ministry of Infrastructure - 4.5 Real Estate Directory

9.11 Trade regulations

The Ministry of Labour, in voting with the affected Ministry of Economy, shall regulate the law of commercial transactions and standing.

The conservation principle applies in the Barter Economy. No more may be sold or exported from the Barter Economy Zone than can grow back in one year. A 75% majority of the population in the Barter Economy Zone must decide on all exports. However, before perishable goods have to be disposed of, they should be sold in the wholesale market .[59]

In Planned Economy, the supply principle applies. Only when all residents of all Social Villages are supported may sales be made into other economic forms. Exceptions are newly established companies that earn their start-up financing with exports in order to open a company in the Social Market Economy or Free Market Economy and to be able to bear the market entry costs, such as premises, inventory or machinery costs.

In the Social Market Economy, the welfare state principle applies. The Planned Economy and Social Market Economy support each other through trade agreements and supplier contracts.

In the Free Market Economy, the principle of free trade applies. The Free Market Economy may trade with all economic forms and international markets, provided that the economic forms or states permit it.

10 Free movement between economic forms[60]

The two mutually exclusive policies, freedom and security, are reconciled by the four ministries of economy and the Ministry of Labour. These ministries ensure that gainful employment and consumption can be chosen by citizens in such a way that a life with more or less freedom or security is possible.

The Ministry of Barter Economy supports a low-cost supply of raw materials without special comforts, but a high degree

---

59 Ministry of Barter Economy - 10.2.2 Wholesale Market
60 §26 Economic freedom: BV Art.27, KV Art.23, §27 Common good
, §153,3 Exclusion of double taxation

of freedom to build, eat, live or work.

The Ministry of Planned Economy provides a minimum supply of goods and services to enjoy the comfort of a life that is 3 decades behind. There is little freedom to decide how to build, eat, live or work, but guaranteed security of supply at all times.

The Ministry of Social Market Economy ensures fair competition through state-guaranteed standards for goods and services and compulsory insurance. Comfort is modest by the standards of the time and rarely allows for luxuries or bankruptcies. Freedom of choice is limited by insurance and standards that guarantee a minimum level of prosperity for all participants.

The Ministry of Free Market Economy ensures global competition without standards as long as they are not set by states in common treaties or laws. Comfort can range from life-threatening poverty to rampant luxury. Freedom of choice is limited only by penal laws and constitutional articles.

The Ministry of Labour ensures that laws regulate the transfer of money, capital and labour between the four economic forms in all areas. It intervenes, if necessary, when one economic form tries to destroy the other through entrepreneurial action. A shortage of labour or consumers, on the other hand, is not entrepreneurial action. The ministries of economy have to make provisions in the law for such occurrences.

10.1 Companies in several economic forms[61]

Each company may only be registered in one economic form. Persons may operate several companies in different economic forms at the same time. Companies may buy or sell in all economic forms if their Ministry of Economy or that of the other economic form does not issue any requirements against it.

For example, a person may rent out a property, invest money in securities, run a service business and work as a part-time worker in a manufacturing company. This person would own

---

61 §215.3 Gainful employment

four companies. The rental company could be registered in the Free Market Economy and subject to its regulations and taxes. The money could be invested in the stock exchanges of the Free Market Economy and Social Market Economy, and thus one financial company could be located in the Social Market Economy and another financial company in the Social Market Economy. The service company could be registered in the Social Market Economy. The production company could be a People's Innovation Company, subject to the labour laws of the Social Market Economy, paying a large part of the profits into the state budget and paying a collectively agreed wage as wages.

10.2 Switching between economic forms[62]

When switching between economic forms, separate rules apply to companies, persons, goods and services. In principle, companies have the right to restructure in order to switch between economic forms. The ministries of economy are responsible for enacting these rules as laws. Should it become necessary for laws to apply equally to all economic forms in order to harmonise switching between economic forms, the Minister of Labour issues these laws in voting with the four Ministers of Economy.

10.2.1 Changing persons

The switching of persons between economic forms takes place through employment and termination with a company of the respective economic form. Every worker and entrepreneur decides on an economic form in which the company is operated. Either the company belongs to him or he works there.

---

62 §219.5 Central Bank and currency policy, §215.3 Gainful employment

10.2.2 Changing companies

Companies can switch between economic forms up to 10 times. Each Ministry of Economy issues its own requirements for switching.[63]

Changing companies is done by changing the setting on the company profile in the Labour Directory. All further steps are displayed. The change can first be simulated. For this purpose, all necessary company data is requested and retrieved from the directory. It is displayed whether and how a change is possible, what changes it entails and how much it costs.

If a company wants to change to another economic form, a special audit must be commissioned from the economic auditors. For each individual case, it is examined whether services could be cheated and standards or levies circumvented. These benefits and levies are priced into the entry fee by the auditors. As part of the special audit, the Company Auditing Agency also checks which standards the company still has to meet in order to obtain approval for the corresponding economic form. The entry fee is increased by the costs incurred to meet all standards. The companies can use this part of the entry fee to meet the standards. It is crucial that the companies can show the money before the change. The Company Auditing Agency checks that the standards are being met accordingly as part of its regular audits.

10.2.3 Changing goods and services

The change of goods and services occurs through the purchase of goods and services from the respective economic form as well as in the multi-market or mono-market. Each consumer decides on the economic form from which goods or services originate when making a purchase. The sale of state-subsidised or paid goods or services from the Social Market Economy to the Free Market Economy is prohibited.

63Ministries of Economy - Switching between economic forms

10.2.3.1 Multimarket

In the multi-market, the assortment must contain the products of all economic forms. By products are meant goods and services. Only if the Barter Economy, due to the conservation principle, and the Planned Economy, due to the supply principle, have end passes or failures in their deliveries, may the products be missing from the assortment. Products of the Social Market Economy may only be missing if no company of the Social Market Economy offers these products in the current season or within a local radius of the inland or 200 kilometres.

Otherwise, all economic forms of a product type must be represented. For example, in a multi-market grocery store there would have to be bread from the Barter Economy, Planned Economy, Social Market Economy and Free Market Economy. All products of an economic form are clearly labelled or presented separately. All products of one product type are presented next to each other or on top of each other. The prices of all products are displayed in all currencies of the country. The customers of the multimarket can pay in all currencies that are accepted as means of payment inland. The multi-market receives a price specification from its providers. The multimarket transfers the amount of the price multiplied by the quantity sold to the providers one day after the sale of the products to its customers. Companies in the Barter Economy and Free Market Economy are paid by the multi-market in the international currency, companies in the Planned Economy and Social Market Economy in the national currency.

Multimarkets are not under the authority of a Ministry of Economy, but of the Ministry of Labour. They must abide by the Social Market Economy's labour laws.

10.2.3.2 Monomarket

Shops that do not want to or cannot offer products from all economic forms in their assortment may only offer products from one economic form. The shops are considered companies of the respective economic form and are subject to the rules of the respective Ministry of Economy.

10.2.4 Citizens' Insurance[64]

Citizens' Insurance allows all state insurance benefits to be pooled. If a move between economic forms takes place, contributions are automatically suspended, Tax-funded or collected. It is possible for private insurance companies to conclude cooperation agreements with Citizens' Insurance. Citizens who change economic form several times during their working life or who work in several companies or several countries and whose companies pay into different pension funds can use Citizens' Insurance. Citizens can choose whether Citizens' Insurance administers all their insurance policies or whether all funds are also invested and earn interest through People's Bank.

In the Barter Economy and Planned Economy, Citizens' Insurance is compulsory and all savings from occupational pension funds must be invested through Citizens' Insurance. 60% of the proceeds from interest accrues to the owners' Barter Economy account and 40% as capital gains tax to the state treasury if the owners live in the Barter Economy or Planned Economy.

10.3 Foreign trade regulations

The Ministry of Labour sets foreign trade regulations in voting with the Ministries of Economy and Foreigners.[65] Foreign trade is regulated to protect the interests of the domestic and foreign economy. To this end, foreign trade may be prohibited, restricted or subject to Customs, which restricts economic freedom. The Ministry of Labour can impose additional regulations on imports and exports from abroad if one economic form damages other economic forms as a result. Together with the ministries of Economy affected and

---

64 §232,1,2c Citizen provision: BV Art. 113
65 Ministries of Economy - Foreign Trade   , Ministry of Foreign Affairs - 7.3.11 International economic policy

the Ministry of Justice, the Ministry of Labour may delete, amend or enact laws of the originating Ministry of Economy for its economic form.

10.3.1 Restrictions[66]

Foreign trade in weapons of war is prohibited, except for trade with states with which there is a defence alliance and a peace treaty.

Barter Economy is subject to an export ban so as not to stress the local natural livelihood beyond its capacity to regenerate.

In the Planned Economy, a balanced or positive foreign trade balance applies, provided that the basic supply of the inhabitants is guaranteed.

The people can obtain a referendum on the export or import of companies or goods with a quorum of 40%. If a quorum of 40% of those entitled to vote is reached, the export of arms and food can be banned for a limited or unlimited period.

The export of foodstuffs is only permitted when domestic demand is saturated. Goods and services that are subsidised by the state may not be exported abroad.

Together with the Ministries of Foreign Affairs, Finance and Economy and the People, the Ministry of Labour negotiates the cross-border purchase and sale of goods, services and companies in trade agreements with other states. The sale of land to foreign companies or persons is prohibited. Leasing is permitted. The sale of domestic government bonds abroad is prohibited.

10.3.2 Tariffs[67]

Tariffs are due for goods, services and companies if the export or import damages the domestic or foreign labour market, environment or health. The requirements for foreign traders are based on the audit results of the Company Auditing Agency. The requirements for domestic citizens are based on

66§225 Foreign trade policy: BV Art. 101
67§152 Tariffs: BV Art.133

the reports on the affected countries. The reports are prepared by the embassies of the Ministry of Foreign Affairs located in the respective foreigner. How high the tariffs are depends on how well the requirements are met. The more damage that can be caused, the higher the tariffs. The amount of damage should correspond to the tariffs in order to be able to compensate for the damage with the revenues. Tariffs not levied by foreigners are collected by the Ministry of Finance. The revenues will only flow to the affected state if its government undertakes to import tariffs in the same amount in the coming year and to spend them on repairing the damage. If the foreigner does not impose such tariffs, the proceeds go into the national treasury, with the recommendation that the revenue be invested in development aid.

11 Labour policy

Labour policy is concerned with how citizens can use their human capital as quickly and easily as possible to earn money. The Ministry of Labour's task is to provide suitable opportunities. Employers and workers can find these opportunities in the Labour Directory. Digitalisation makes it possible to automate search processes and not miss a single moment when windows of opportunity open up for transfer in the labour market. In business practice, employers offer jobs, employees offer their labour and companies offer goods, services and innovations. All these offers can be found on profiles in the Labour Directory.

11.1 Reconciliation of work and private life

To promote work-life balance, the Ministry of Labour offers the election between four economic forms and within them the possibilities to adapt work to private life and not vice versa. In the Barter Economy and Free Market Economy, those who value free self-determination and what role their work life or private life will play have the freedom of choice, but no certainty that this will happen. In Planned Economy there is compulsory work for basic supply available to all residents and the rest is free time. In the Social Market Economy there are compulsory insurances, rights and obligations for employers and employees to take care of each other and to trust with certainty that it will turn out that way.

11.2 Vocational education[68]

The Ministry of Labour coordinates the regularisation of vocational training with the Ministries of Education, Economy and Innovation. The Ministry of Education provides education and training for skilled workers. The ministries of economy are the representations of the companies of their economic form. They are responsible for ensuring that the companies can pass on their needs to the educational institutions. This can be done through small official channels, with entrepreneurs visiting the heads of the educational institutions or vice versa. However, if the overall situation is to change, the responsible Ministry of Economy arranges for a discussion with the Ministry of Labour, quasi the large official channels. If no quick solution can be found because too many people are affected, the Ministry of Labour will appeal to the ministers of education, economy and innovation to formulate innovations and submit them to the people for a vote.

11.2.1 Necessary educational content[69]

The Ministry of Labour, in voting with the Ministries of Education and Innovation, provides curricula, in-service training and final exams. To ensure that the skilled workers are suitable to find work in the economy, the Ministry of Education, in voting with the Ministries of Labour and Innovation, determines the basic content of the final examinations and works in cooperation with companies. The final examinations of the educational institutions are designed in such a way that graduates can pursue the appropriate appeal

68§181.3 Vocational training, §215.2 Gainful employment: BV Art. 95
69§177,2 Education, §180,2,3 Schools and colleges: BV Art. 63a,
§215,2 Gainful employment: BV Art. 95

throughout the country.[70]

In voting with the Ministry of Labour, the Ministry of Education prepares curricula for comprehensive schools and all secondary colleges. The curricula are to be geared towards preparing learners for the final examinations and working life in the best possible way.[71]

11.2.2 Practical work

In order to promote vocational education within the framework of an ongoing education and employment system, elements with practical work are built into all specialisations of the educational institutions.[72] The Company Auditing Agency is responsible for cooperation with the companies within the framework of its audits of the companies and educational institutions. The cooperation includes partial production of individual parts for companies in the classroom, visits of working people to the appropriate subject, visits of school classes to companies, work placements and in-service training periods. The educational institutions and their staff can either connect with the companies themselves, or they commission the Employment Office to offer them suitable companies for cooperation. The same applies to companies seeking cooperation with educational institutions.

Companies of all economic forms are required to participate in in-service training for the purpose of training promotion. To provide training, companies with vacant training positions must offer internships. In these internships, interns and companies should become clear whether their expectations are being met and whether in-service training should follow. As part of its audits, the Company Auditing Agency ensures that companies with suitable job profiles are matched with suitable specialisations at educational institutions. The Institute for Education[73] investigates which sectors and

---

70 Ministry of Education - 9.19 Final examinations, 11.6.8 Higher education degrees
71 Ministry of Education - 4.4.2 Curriculum development
72 Ministry of Education - 4.9.2 Cooperation between educational institutions and companies
73 Ministry of Education - 4.7 Institute of Education

companies with which specialisations and educational levels are the best match and communicates this to the Company Auditing Agency. The Institute for Education is responsible for continuously identifying all companies in the vicinity of educational institutions that would be suitable for teaching. For this purpose, the Institute uses the data of the Company Auditing Agency.

11.2.3 Practical research

The Ministry of Innovation ensures that the industries of the future, in which the level of research and development is high, receive sufficient skilled workers. It ensures that the research institutions cooperate with the educational institutions.[74] The research institutions consist of researching companies and institutes. The participating educational institutions are all comprehensive schools and colleges. The companies can conduct research in educational institutions after their class hours, use the inventory and pay a cost-covering share for the operating costs. Learners can be authorised by the company to observe or participate. Educational institutions can participate in comparative research and studies to test and develop innovations to market more quickly.

12 Employment Office

The Employment Office is responsible for placement activities in the labour market. The head of the Employment Office is an elected politician. The Employment Office keeps labour market statistics with data from the Company Auditing Agency, which allows it to examine past upturns and downturns in the economy and make predictions for future development. Based on this ongoing monitoring and analysis of the labour market, the Employment Office provides employment exchange services in cooperation with the ministries of business, innovation, education, media and digital.

74Ministry of Education - 4.10 Education through research

12.1 Passive labour market promotion[75]

Passive labour market promotion consists of measures that enable citizens to survive periods of their lives without gainful employment unscathed. The Employment Office pursues the goal of full employment by placing jobseekers in the labour market of at least one economic form. If a jobseeker cannot find a job in the Barter Economy, Free Market Economy and Free Market Economy, he or she can live as a homeless person or move into a Social Village.

12.1.1 Life in the Planned Economy

Temporary accommodation for unemployed nationals is provided by the Ministry of Planned Economy. The unemployed nationals are not forced to move to Social Villages. They have the right to do so, but not the obligation. The Planned Economy is obliged to take in all unemployed nationals of the other three economic forms. In return, the Ministry of Planned Economy receives compensation payments[76] per capita from the ministries of economy from which the unemployed come in order to adjust the capacity in the Social Villages. The economic form from which one comes depends on where the company is or was registered that generated the person's highest income in the previous year and the person was terminated or the company was closed. The Ministry of Labour provides laws that allow for involuntary moves to the Social Village due to financial hardship. These laws regulate labour market issues of special groups of people, namely the unemployed, the disabled and underfunded pensioners.

The Planned Economy provides a minimum level of welfare to all nationals at all times and indefinitely. The welfare ensures that at least a dry and warm bed, three meals a day, a clean body, clean clothes, essential health care, free education and enjoyable recreational opportunities are provided.

---

75 §228.8 Labour: KV Art.39
76 Ministry of Planned Economy   - 16.3.4 Compensation payments

12.1.2 Precaution[77]

The Ministry of Labour facilitates precautionary measures for So-called special groups of people. These are the unemployed, survivors, the elderly and the disabled. The Ministry of Labour obliges the Ministries of Planned Economy and Social Market Economy to establish two pillars of provision. The Ministry of Planned Economy enables needy nationals to benefit from the services provided in the Social Villages at any time and for an unlimited period.[78] The Ministry of Social Market Economy provides unemployment insurance and pension insurance for all residents.[79] Companies in the Social Market Economy must pay 50% of the contributions of employees and entrepreneurs into these compulsory insurances. The remaining 50% comes from employees' wages and entrepreneurs' profits. The third pillar of pension provision is the self-provision of all persons. It is supported by the possibility of investing money in the savings account, pension account and generation account at People's Bank.[80]

12.1.2.1 Old and survivors

Nationals who are of retirement age but whose pension is not sufficient to survive have the right to move into a Social Village. They can continue to receive their pension benefits, but must pay the Planned Economy corporate tax rate on them.

Orphans are placed in the children's houses of the Social Villages and, if possible, placed with foster parents. Widows and widowers whose deceased partner had provided income can move into the Social Village house for senior citizens or unmated persons, depending on their age.

---

77 §229.1 Unemployment, old-age, survivors' and disability benefits: BV Art. 111
78 Ministry of Planned Economy - 17.1 Social welfare
79 Ministry of Social Market Economy - 17.5.4 Pension insurance, 17.5.3 Unemployment insurance
80 Ministry of Finance - 11.5.6 Pension Account, 11.5.4 Savings Account, 11.5.7 Generation Account

12.1.2.2 Disabled[81]

Humans with chronic diseases, mental or physical disabilities are examined in university hospitals. There, the severity of the disability, the So-called degree of disability, is recorded as a percentage and a disability certificate is issued, which indicates which disabilities are present and how severe they are. The Institute for Occupational Health, in cooperation with the examining university clinics, determines which occupation can still be carried out with which disability and to what extent.[82]

The Ministry of Labour obliges the Ministries of Planned Economy and Social Market Economy to integrate disabled people into their labour markets. Disabled persons who are still fully able to carry out certain executive activities are given preference in the allocation of jobs in Social Market Economy companies if they are equally qualified. Disabled persons who are no longer able to carry out gainful employment are admitted to homes for the disabled in the Social Villages, where they are looked after and cared for until their death.[83] If it is possible, simple work should be done in homes for the disabled that the residents are capable of doing. Disabled people have the right to move into state homes for the disabled, but not the obligation. Especially if their relatives want to accommodate, care for and look after them at their own expense, they can do so.

12.2 Active labour market promotion

Active labour market promotion consists of measures that promote rapid integration into any labour market. It is subject to costs, which each year must answer financial labour market policy questions for the previous and coming year in the annual budget vote. The measures listed below are subject to this funding requirement.

To promote employment and self-employment, the

---

81 §231 Integration of disabled persons: BV Art. 112b
82 Ministry of Health - 4.5.5 Institute of Occupational Health, 5.6.1 University Hospitals
83 Ministry of Planned Economy - 18.1.6 House for disabled people

Employment Office maintains the Labour Directory. The economic forms can offer their own support measures. The Ministry of Planned Economy must ensure at least the possibility of an Experimental Enterprise or Innovation Enterprise in the Social Villages.[84]

To get a non-binding impression of a company or an intern, the Employment Office pays the minimum wage of interns at 60%.

In the event of an economic downturn, the Ministry of Labour, in voting with the Ministry of Finance, can pay money from the Economic Cycle Compensation Fund[85] to employees of the companies. All employees receive payments to cover 60% of their last monthly income over the following 6 months. The numbers of the last rate can be adjusted by the Ministry of Labour to the severity of the downturn and the amount of savings available.

12.2.1 Employment exchange[86]

The Employment Office offers employment exchange services to employers and employees, primarily through the Labour Directory. In addition to this digital service, recruiters provide professional guidance in handling the Labour Directory and match employers with suitable employees and vice versa. Personnel consultants offer an extended service that supports employers and employees from the search and application process to the end of the probationary period.

For the best possible employment exchange, all companies are obliged by the Employment Office to report their vacancies in the Labour Directory. The Ministry of Education will be obliged to establish sufficient capacities in all educational programmes in which there is a labour shortage in all economic forms, although the working conditions are above average.

84Ministry of Planned Economy - 10.8 Experimental Enterprises, 10.6 Innovation Enterprises
85Ministry of Finance - 7.5 Balancing the business cycles
86§215,4 Gainful employment, §233,1,2 Unemployment placement: BV Art.114

12.2.1.1 Recruiter

The recruiters are Employment Office staff from the local town hall. They conduct regular career counselling sessions at the Intranet Café. This quick initial consultation is an introduction to the Labour Directory and the professional entry of all personal data and search requests. This helps to determine whether there is a shortage of appropriate workers or skilled workers in an economic form and which of these jobs the jobseeker would like to fill. If further education is required for a desired appeal, the jobseeker can use all educational institutions to obtain the desired qualification. Through classroom visits, learners are taught how to use the Labour Directory by recruiters before their final examinations.

12.2.1.2 Personnel consultant

Employers or employees can engage the personnel consultants of the Employment Office. The employment service is chargeable to the principal. The personnel consultants work with the Company Auditing Agency's business consultants and access the Company Auditing Agency's data set. They undertake the placement of highly qualified workers for a specific post in a specific company. The personnel consultants test the personality, interests, knowledge and skills of the candidates. With the data obtained, they specifically search for companies that fit the person. Several candidates are proposed to the company and several companies are proposed to the candidates. Once the recruitment is completed, the personnel consultants' remuneration follows. They receive 30% of an annual salary, payable over 5 years.

Personnel consultants plan the person's career path with them. Applications are prepared as a portfolio and file with application video, interviews are prepared, rehearsed and followed up. Depending on the orders, the interview and qualification tests are also taken over for the company, so that the company only has to select one candidate. The personnel consultant accompanies the person until the end of the probationary period.

12.2.1.3 Support for business start-ups

The Employment Office supports jobseekers in setting up a company. Recruiters conduct a market analysis with the founders via the Labour Directory and test demand and the optimal location. The personnel consultants can put together a suitable team of skilled workers for each start-up and, if necessary, poach skilled workers from other companies. In Planned Economy, all nationals have the right to start an Experimental Enterprise or an Innovation Enterprise. The Ministry of Planned Economy will be obliged to provide Social Villagers and interested entrepreneurs with the opportunity to consult the expertise of other Social Village residents in order to recruit them as staff or part of the entrepreneurial community. The Ministry of Planned Economy will provide follow-up and may provide financial support for the establishment of an Experimental Enterprise or an Innovation Enterprise if necessary.[87]

12.2.2 Further education[88]

Further education is a measure that builds on qualifications that have already been successfully completed and makes it possible for all age groups to achieve any higher qualification. The Ministry of Education is responsible for continuing education.[89] The ministries of labour, economy and innovation, in voting with the Ministry of Education, determine which further education measures are to be offered where and when. The Company Auditing Agency, through the auditors for business, innovation and technology, collects the data of all persons and companies seeking further education measures and forwards it to the Ministry of Education. The Ministry of Education provides the measures and invites the persons affected to the educational institution for classes or final exams. Distance learning and face-to-face learning are offered. For distance learning, the Ministry of Education cooperates

87 Ministry of Planned Economy - 10.8 Experimental Enterprises, 10.6 Innovation Enterprises
88 §182 Continuing education: BV Art. 64a
89 Ministry of Education - 12 Free Education

with the Ministries of Media and Digital Affairs to digitise the further education measures. All further education measures can be accessed in the Knowledge Directory .[90]

All unemployed nationals can choose a Social Village through the Employment Office where the training they want is offered and move in. The Employment Office organises the move with the Social Service.[91] In the Social Villages, all residents receive employment in basic supply. If the job seekers have sufficient means, they do not have to move into the Social Village but can commute.

12.2.3 Education fairs

Once a year, the Employment Office organises fairs in educational submissions after graduation, where employers from the surrounding area run a stand. The Employment Office invites all companies that have a scheduled vacancy or already have a vacancy within the next year. Companies looking for trainees for in-service training already advertise them in the comprehensive school. The Employment Office, together with the Ministry of Education, arranges classroom visits by entrepreneurs and staff, training fairs at comprehensive schools and visits by pupils to companies. The training fairs take place in the 11th and 12th learning year before the pupils take their lower secondary or advanced qualification.[92]

12.2.4 Intern Party

The Employment Office organises intern parties at local educational institutions or community centres. Once there are more than 50 interns in a city, all interns in the city are invited once a month via the Labour Directory. Entrance is free. Food and drinks are available at cost price, but you can also bring your own.

The purpose of these parties is to network interns and their bosses. Bosses should give their interns business cards of

90 Ministry of Education - 12.7 Knowledge Directory
91 Ministry of Planned Economy - 9.4.1 Social Service
92 Ministry of Education - 9.18 Final years 11 to 13

themselves to exchange with suitable interns from suitable companies. Interns can also exchange their own business cards or contact details directly. Interns get to talk to each other through a get-to-know-you table. Speed dating is offered there all the time, where people talk for 2 minutes until they change their counterpart on a rotating basis. The aim is for interns to exchange information about the intersections of their activities and to collect presumably interesting contact addresses that could be useful for the company or the interns. Interns can share what they think about different companies, which ones they recommend or rather not. This should make it easier for interns to find the right job for them.

At each party there is another get-to-know table for unmated persons and stickers in the shape of hearts with numbers. Each unmated person can take a sticker and visibly attach it to themselves or sit at the get-to-know table. Employees of the interns who are unmated persons are allowed to accompany the interns.

12.2.5 Job rotation

The Employment Office offers internship contracts remunerated at the Social Market Economy minimum wage for 1 year. Up to 12 internships can be completed during this year. The applicants can choose their own jobs or they can use proposals that an algorithm creates for them personally based on their profile in the Labour Directory. The Employment Office has the right to prescribe up to 3 months of internships in certain workplaces in the programme of job rotation. These can be domestic companies on the verge of losing money, Non-profit enterprises or state enterprises.

12.2.6 Transfer agreement for older employees

There are occupations that cannot be exercised until retirement age. The Institute of Occupational Health and the health auditors of the Company Auditing Agency track down gentle and stressful occupations and up to what age they can be practised safely and profitably. Employees and entrepreneurs are interviewed in surveys.

Employees are asked to assess whether they think they will be able to work in their profession until they retire or until what age they can work in their profession. If an occupation cannot be carried out until retirement, workers are asked to indicate in which occupation they could imagine working afterwards.

Entrepreneurs are to assess up to what age their appeal and that of their employees can be exercised. The company data is used to check how productive employees of different ages are in the various jobs in the company.

This data is used to find companies and sectors that are more attractive for young or old workers. The Employment Office ensures that takeover agreements are concluded between companies. The economic auditors of the Company Auditing Agency contact companies via the Labour Directory that have been indicated by interviewed entrepreneurs and workers, have been assessed as suitable by industry associations or employers' and workers' associations. In the case of a takeover agreement, employees know in advance which company they will continue to work for at an advanced age. When the transfer takes place depends on the one hand on the employees and their desire, and on the other hand on the acquiring company, if and when a position becomes vacant there because workers retire or give notice.

In the case of takeover agreements, care should be taken to ensure that, if possible, no further training is necessary or that only a small amount of content needs to be relearned for the new job and that old experience can be used. The Labour Directory profile of a company shows the companies that have a transfer agreement with this company. In the career planner, job changes and suitable companies are automatically proposed.

If necessary, the Ministry of Labour, in voting with the ministries of economy, can also impose age quotas in certain companies so that, for example, 60% of employees must be over 50 years old. Transfer agreements must be concluded between state enterprises if the Institute of Occupational Health finds occupations in state enterprises that are burdensome for older workers.

13 Labour Directory

The Labour Directory is the central platform on the intranet that lists the supply and demand of goods, services, jobs and workers for the entire country. It also serves as a trade and business register. Workers and their qualifications as well as companies and their goods and services on offer are presented as profiles.

In the Labour Register, every person who lives inland and is of employable age is given a profile as a worker. Employer, employee and unemployed are only the status in which a profile is located. The Labour Directory is an interactive intranet platform linked to other directories and programmes of the Ministry of Digital Affairs. It is designed to allow people to talk, communicate and network with colleagues to form groups such as workplace sports, employers' associations, works councils or labour unions for bargaining groups.

In order to search for more efficient and innovative products and production methods, entire workforces in their sectors can search for solutions together. Through networking, solution paths become visible that individual companies use but other companies did not know about before. Companies can discuss future developments and research projects in groups. On the one hand, private individuals present themselves on the digital job market with their picture and CV. On the other hand, there are profiles of companies that are cared for by the departments for purchasing, sales and human resources in order to digitally present the company's supply and demand for products and labour. Users can always see who has visited their profile and which profiles they themselves have visited. The Labour Directory is thus a mixture of the well-known internet platforms such as facebook[93] , linkedin[94] , stepstone[95] , wlw (Who supplies what)[96] and amazon[97] . The administration

---

93https://www.facebook.com/
94https://www.linkedin.com/
95https://www.stepstone.com/
96https://www.wlw.de/en/home
97https://www.amazon.com/

of companies via the profile in the Labour Directory is offered by software similar to SAP[98] via servers of the Ministry of Digital Affairs with which companies are connected via the intranet.

13.1 Profiles for persons

Every nationals has a profile as a worker from the age of legal capacity. Personal data, such as name, age, sex and place of residence, are retrieved from the profile in the Persons Directory[99]. The degrees and visits to education are retrieved from the profile in the Education Directory[100]. Each user can decide which data is displayed on their profile in the Labour Directory and hide what is not displayed.

On the profile page, the user can set whether he is currently looking for a new job, regardless of whether he is currently employed by a company or not. Accordingly, his or her labour with his or her skills will be listed in the search results that are shown to employers who are looking. Employers can be companies, private individuals or other entrepreneurial persons who want to start a company and are looking for skilled workers as founding members.

No matter what company a worker is in, their profile should be the digital personnel file to replace paper-based administration. When one joins a company, the company gets additional viewing rights, rights to use certain data and writing rights for the areas of the digital personnel file. When one leaves the company, these rights expire again for the company. You take your digital personnel file with you, including all your own and other person's entries. Entries created by the company in the digital personnel file cannot be changed by the owner of the profile, but cannot be displayed to other users.

---

98 https://www.sap.com/about.html
99 Ministry of State Organisation - 4.6 Persons Directory
100 Ministry of Education - 5.9 Education Directory

13.2 Profiles for companies

Companies can be administered via their profile. Entrepreneurs can make use of this service, but do not have to. However, certain company data must be entered into the profile in order to be audited by the Company Auditing Agency. The Company Auditing Agency sends a notice to all entrepreneurs who do not administer their companies via the profile in the Labour Directory in good time before its audit. The State administers companies only through the Labour Directory. For each new business profile created, a tax account is automatically created with the People's Bank through which business taxes are paid. All enterprise data is used for state statistics, employment exchange and economic planning by the ministries of economy. In addition, the algorithm of the Algoracle[101] accesses the data to simulate future effects of deciders.

13.2.1 Setting up a business

As soon as a person wants to set up a company, all he or she has to do is create a profile in the Labour Directory. Mandatory details are name, address, industry and the type of service provided by the company. The person who creates the profile is registered as the owner of the company by default. The personal details are automatically retrieved from the Persons Directory. If a company has more than one owner, their profiles must be searched for and inserted in the Labour Directory. Co-owners must confirm this action before they are displayed in the company's profile. All persons working for the company are displayed as workers.

No matter what activity earns money, a new company profile must be created for it. The activity must be specified and is listed in a selection menu as soon as the activity is described in the input field. If the activity is already listed, the appropriate keywords can be selected. If the activity is not listed, it can be created and is then available in the list of activities.

For example, anyone who invests their money with People's

---

101 Ministry of Digital Affairs - 15.3 Algoracle

Bank automatically opens a company with the activity "investment of money" in the Social Market Economy.

When drawing up a company profile, the economic form in which the company is to operate must be selected. This decides the responsibility of the responsible Ministry of Economy and which rules the company management should follow.

13.2.2 Digital marketing

Companies indicate via their profile page which goods or services they supply. Customers can contact the companies directly via a messaging function. Companies can also process orders via an integrated digital shop. The application can be activated by a click in the settings. Layout, videos, photos and descriptions are automatically proposed and can be selected, added to or replaced. The web shop automatically taxes profits or sales and transfers the profits to the company.

Using an algorithm, all buyers in the market can be located, where they are and what quantity they would buy at what prices.

13.2.3 Work programme

Work scheduling can be done through the Labour Directory and is a Tax-funded offering of the Ministry of Labour. Democratic duty rosters, digitised administration and the networked management of machines can be carried out with the help of the work programme. Similar to oversized People's Computers, the servers are located in the companies and are stored there in a decentralised manner, but are connected to the intranet. Just as people's data resides on the person's People's Computer, companies' data resides on their servers, which they can buy or rent from the Intranet Café. Companies also have the right to use the central servers of the Ministry of Digital Affairs. For this, however, they get a cost-covering fee plus 10% profit deducted via the tax account.

With the help of the programme, duty rosters can be created digitally and their operation simulated virtually. Faults in the duty roster are thus avoided, even if it is created democratically among all the participants. If employees have to work overtime, this is automatically recorded and taken into account in the upcoming duty roster. Working time models such as flexitime, part-time and working from home are made easier by the digital duty roster, but only employees of the Social Market Economy are entitled to this. Otherwise, it is up to the parties to the employment contract to agree on such regularisations or not.

The programme is also capable of handling all digital operations, especially digitised administration. It is the software that is programmed by the Ministry of Digital Affairs for all ministries and state enterprises anyway. If companies also want to use this programme with open source code, they can do so free of charge. In return, however, they are required to report faults in the programme and, if possible, to create alternative solutions in the source code and send them to the Ministry of Digital Affairs. Through the programme, the auditors of the Company Auditing Agency can audit the company more quickly and thus more cheaply. Users of the programme receive all automatically recognised suggestions for improvement free of charge in the audit report for each audit.

13.3 Innovation marketing

Every patent and every other industrial property right granted by the Patent Office[102] as well as saleable entries in the Innovation Database[103] automatically receive a profile. There, it is recorded which companies use the industrial property right or who pays licence fees to the inventor(s). Interested investors, entrepreneurs or other customers can use the search function to find innovations that could be useful for their company and approach inventors via the profile. Business ideas are also considered innovations and can be tested via digital demand.

---

102 Ministry of Innovation - 7.3 Patent Office
103 Ministry of Innovation - 9.7 Innovation Database

13.3.1 Digital demand

Through the Labour Directory, citizens can register a need for something. For example, if citizens would like to have a restaurant in their town, they can set it up virtually. As soon as a sufficient number of users also follow this need, an algorithm creates a corresponding company profile that automatically searches for interested and qualified owners and employees and proposes that they open the company.

13.3.2 Innovation Database

On the Innovation Database, trade secrets are notarised so that it is clear who had an innovation first. The data transfer takes place via the People's Computer of a company owner, or the owner of the trade secret. The data exchange takes place via an extra encrypted line to a secured separate server. The use of this storage service is voluntary and financed within the framework of the business tax. The Innovation Database itself is operated by the Ministry of Innovation, but is available via the Labour Directory.

13.4 Homepage

The start page can be designed by the user by arranging all control fields from the columns individually in all columns and positions. The header contains the intranet address of the page. The web address "in" stands for "intranet", followed by the name of the page and the folder path of the intranet pages on the servers. Below the input bar for the intranet address, job offers are displayed as advertisements that match the user's personal data. At the bottom of the page, advertisements for industrial property rights, goods and services listed in the Labour Directory are displayed.

13.4.1 News service

At the top of the left column, the message service is displayed. The "message service" can send files such as text, sound recordings, pictures and videos to all users of the intranet. It is available in all directories and has its own mailbox for the Labour Directory.

13.4.2 Security settings

The "Security Settings" allow you to administer the visibility or invisibility of all data for specific users and contacts. The security settings have a function that simulates the view of the profile by a stranger, a friend, a colleague or a specific group of people.

13.4.3 Photos & Videos

"Photos & Videos" are representations of work done that can be displayed on the profile page.

13.4.4 Working groups

"Working groups" are all groups in which a worker is active in order to carry out an activity regulated by himself or herself or by others, voluntarily or professionally, with other workers.

13.4.5 Colleagues

"Colleagues" are all the colleagues the user has ever had in their working life. The jobs and activities each colleague has performed and how the user has dealt with the colleague in the workflow are displayed. The assignment is made by an algorithm that analyses the job descriptions. If a colleague is no longer working together with the user, the work he or she is currently doing is displayed, provided the visibility of this data has been released by the colleague. Each user can sort their colleagues into specially defined categories. Preset categories are how well you know a colleague, which data you want to share with them and which you do not.

13.4.6 Superior

"Superiors" are all the superiors the user has ever had in their working life. Here, too, the algorithm calculates the assignment in the workflow based on the organisational chart and the job description and shows the superior's current job. Users can also create categories here to sort their superiors by position.

13.4.7 Memberships

"Memberships" are all memberships in clubs, unifications and groups listed in the Labour Directory. From company sports to further education and labour unions, all organisations are listed here that serve to make work healthier, more educated and fairer.

13.4.8 Company

"Companies" are all companies where the user has ever worked. The list is automatically created as soon as a company fills the user for an advertised position. In the display, these are the profile pages of the companies. For digital administration, only the current company is authorised to use the user's profile for their personnel file. All entries made by the company in an employee's personnel file are stored on their profile and are thus visible to the affected user. Entries from past companies are no longer visible to subsequent companies. The visibility of the personnel file is only enabled for the personnel department and the user, but can be extended by the user. If the user runs a company himself, everything he wants to publish about himself will be displayed. If the company has a personnel department and the user as owner has a personnel file, his or her entries from the personnel department are displayed.

13.4.9 Career planner

The Career Planner is a programme for users of the Labour Directory to enter various appeals they plan to make in their lives. Using a timeline from their current age to their pension, users can enter dates or periods of time in which a change of occupation is to take place. It is possible to enter several appeals, which can split the career path and have several branches. Which branch or diversions is taken on the timeline is decided by chance on the one hand, when a desired job becomes available or whether it becomes available on the specified date. On the other hand, the user decides when to accept the programme's offers and find out about the company or apply. The programme continuously searches all specified appeals in a certain radius or in several radii and reports the vacancies to the user via news. Users can set whether and when they want to receive news about which occupations.

The career planner indicates if further educational qualifications are necessary for a selected appeal. A linker shows where and when the user can obtain the qualification, whether and which options exist for in-service training and which alternatives take how long.

Users can publish the information from the career planner on their profile so that companies can better plan which employees would take which next step in their professional career and when companies should advertise new jobs. The user can hide the advertisement on their profile, like all other data, from all or certain other users.

13.4.10 Past visitors

The left column ends with the persons who last viewed the user's profile, when and for how long they viewed, commented or rated what on which pages of the profile.

13.4.11 News

In the centre, all contributions from colleagues, superiors, organisations, companies and working groups are displayed in chronological or algorithmic order in a small window at the very top. The user can switch whether only posts from certain or all colleagues, superiors, organisations, companies or working groups are displayed. The user can switch whether the posts should be sorted chronologically since the last visit or whether an algorithm should be switched on to filter posts that might interest the user. The user can view the settings of the algorithm and adjust them for himself.

If there is a new news item in the Labour Directory mailbox, the report "You have new mail" is displayed. If a company, group or organisation has a message for all participants involved, the report "You have a video message" is displayed, provided the message is a video. If a visitor to the profile page sends a greeting to the user, the report "You have been greeted" is displayed. If a user is invited to an open or closed group, the report "You have been invited to the group "[name of group]"." If a new colleague wants to join the user's network and has sent a request, the report "You have a new colleague request" is displayed. All colleagues with whom a user is currently working are automatically added to the user's colleague network. If the user leaves the company, all past colleagues also disappear from the network, unless they had already connected through a colleague request. If an organisation wants to suggest the user to join, the report "You have been invited to [type of organisation and name]" will appear. If a company has selected the user for a vacancy and wants to meet them, the report "You have been invited for an interview" will appear. Through the messaging service, the interview can also be conducted by video. If the user has the expertise to fill a corresponding order that another user has to place, the report "You have a new order request" appears.

The bottom of the central column shows which companies have visited the user's profile, when and how.

13.4.12 Daily news

At the very top of the right-hand column, the daily news is displayed. The user can choose whether they should be shown in the form of text, sound, picture or video, how long the news should last in total and which sections should be informed about. The categories are, for example, company start-ups, patent applications, the economy, politics, sport, weather, culture and fun.

13.4.13 Search

The search function in the middle of the right-hand column allows the user to search the Labour Directory for different profiles and keywords.

Keywords are assigned by all users when they create their profile. Keywords that do not exist yet but are entered are stored in a database. As soon as such a keyword has been entered 100 times, the site operator checks whether the keyword can be linked to other keywords or whether a new keyword must be assigned to a category.

A radius around a specific address can be defined in the search settings. Search results can be further narrowed down in terms of time and subject.

For each search category, there is a search bar and a tab with a scrollable list of keywords or search terms that match the previous entry. Categories can be searched by industry, company, experience, person, group or help. It is possible for the user to link search results from the different categories. This makes it possible, for example, to search for groups in which persons who are members of the group have certain experiences and work or have worked in a certain industry. Experiences are keywords that are assigned to qualifications of professionals. Users can search for persons or companies with these experiences, or educational institutions that offer these experiences in training courses. The Ministry of Education checks keywords given by companies and persons to describe qualifications and links them to educational programmes offered by the Ministry of Education. The same applies to goods and services, which can be sorted by price, proximity of reference and Company Auditing Agency audit results.

The search results can be displayed in a list or a tree diagram. The tree diagram shows industries to which companies belong, where persons with certain experience work or goods and services with certain certified characteristics are present. The list can be sorted alphabetically, chronologically, locally or by subject.

13.4.14 Administrator news

News from the site operator to the user is displayed under the search windows, as is the imprint and a link to a contact form to the site operator in the Ministry of Digital Affairs. The total number of users who have a profile, who are in "unemployed" status, who are currently online, and the number of companies that are currently online, have vacancies and free capacities are also displayed there.

13.4.15 Example

The start page of the Labour Directory is listed here as an example for a worker living in the Rhine-Main area. The links are shown on the start page. Selecting the link displays the content described above.

Header:
Web address: din.arbeitsvz.de/mystartpage/
MariusMustermann1986
Advertising: We are looking for industrial clerks in the Rhine-Main area for 2500 Euro basic salary!

Footer:
Advertising: Buy the patented universal cutter for 19.99 euros! We clean your living space in the Offenbach district for 1.99 euros per square metre!

Left column	Centre	Right column
My profile page	Your superior Moritz Mustermann is on sick leave for a week.	Daily News [Video] in 100 seconds
News service	-> You have new mail	Search industry
Security settings	-> You have a video message	Search company
My Photos & Videos	-> You were greeted	Search experiences
My working groups	-> You have been invited to join the „We are SIEMENS" group.	Search persons
My colleagues	-> You have a new colleague request	Search groups
My superiors	-> You have been invited to join a labour union	Search help
My member-ships	-> You have been invited for an interview	Contact Imprint Server will be down today from 0-4 for maintenance work
My company My career path	-> You have a new order request	Total members: 55 432 100 Of which unemployed: 1 156 258
Max Muster (colleague 2001-2005) visited your page on 12/05/2018 for 7 minutes. [Show details]	Siemens viewed your page on 10/05/2018 for 12 minutes. [Show details]	Persons currently online: 12 345 678 Company currently online: 2 345 678

13.5 Profile page

On the profile page, users enter the information they would like to publish in order to earn money with their labour, their company or their innovation. They are supported by the algorithm, which automatically enters all the data that is available on the intranet about the user. All entries are linked to keywords that other users can then search for. Keywords are categorised and assigned to industries, companies, education and research institutions.

13.5.1 Page layout

The header contains the intranet address of the page. The path after "arbeitsvz.de/" indicates whether the profile is of a person, a company or an innovation, followed by the name of the person, company or innovation. Users who visit a profile page are shown advertisements at the top and bottom of the page that match the characteristics of the profile owner.
The profile picture can be seen at the top left and the name can be read above it. The profile picture is a portrait or full-body photo for persons, the logo and location for companies, and the image of the innovation for innovations. To the right, a cover picture, video, text or an interactive simulation can be placed in the middle. On the right are the contact details and address of the company, person or inventor. Below the profile picture are the facts of the profile.
Under the title picture in the middle, work samples and the current view from the career planner are displayed for persons, an order page (webshop) for companies or intended uses for innovations. The content can be displayed as text, image, sound, video or interactive simulation.
Each profile is completed by the pinboard, where the user and other users authorised by the user can leave posts, comments and replies.[104]

---

104 Ministry of Digital Affairs - 12.8 Post, comment and reply

13.5.2 Contents of persons

For persons, the left-hand side shows age, interests, current occupation, career aspirations, degrees, further education, past work experience, digital expertise in devices and programmes and other qualifications. For vocational and educational qualifications, it shows where they were taken and how long the experience lasted. An algorithm automatically imports all existing data from other directories. Users can determine which information they want to show to whom, which they want to add or hide.

For persons, the right-hand side displays the working groups, colleagues, superiors, memberships and companies listed in the user's contact network. Clicking on the link displays a list of contacts that can be sorted by name, age, chronology, industry or skill.

13.5.3 Company contents

For companies, the left-hand side shows the industry, the age, the past annual turnover, the head office and, if applicable, other locations, the goods or services offered, the required qualifications for employees, the benefits for customers, the responsible trade union for employees, the responsible employers' association and in which economic form the company is registered.

Companies that want to offer their goods or services via the order page in the Labour Directory indicate opening hours, shipping options and payment methods there. The easiest way to pay is via the intranet. Users who visit the site with their People's Computer or in the intranet café can pay via their People's Bank account. The amount is automatically collected via the People's Bank current account or via the tax account from the specified bank.

For companies, the number of employees is displayed under the contact data on the right-hand side, when employees will retire again and how many positions will be vacant next. A linker can be used to call up a calendar for the coming year, showing which vacancies need to be filled and when.

If companies are administered digitally via the profile, all information from the digital personnel files is automatically retrieved and updated. For each company that permanently employs staff, a linker displays the company's organisation chart, showing how many staff are currently employed and when positions become vacant due to age or according to the career planner. If a company has takeover agreements with other companies, these companies are listed via a linker.

13.5.4 Contents of innovations

For innovations, the left-hand side shows the age, the inventor(s), the industry or industries, companies already using the innovation, the past annual turnover generated by the innovation and what other opportunities, industries or companies could benefit from the innovation.
For innovations, the right-hand side displays the industries, associations, companies, markets, research and educational institutions where the innovation is or could be used or offered. Clicking on the link displays a list that can be sorted by sectors, associations, companies, markets, research and educational institutions, as well as current, past and potential users.

13.5.5 Example

Intranet address: din.labour.dir/
[person,company,innovation]/name

Name & profile picture	Cover picture / Video	Contact details
Facts about	*Text, image, sound, video or interactive simulation*	*Networks and links to other profiles*
- Person - Company	- Work samples, career path - Webshop	- professional & personal contact networks - Employees, vacancies, takeover agreements - Past, present & potential clients
- Innovation	- Uses	

Directory: Labour Directory	Ministry: Ministry of Labour

Post, comment or reply: Title

Image	Name	Keyword Coordinate System[1]	Date

Content of the news (text, sound, image, video)

+	-	!	B	K	A	<3	:D	:0	:(	:((
For this	Against this	Mark & Cite Key-word Coordinate System	Create post	Comments	Create answer	In love	Amused	Amazed	Sad	Angry

85

13.6 Algorithm for the search for workers and jobs

The Labour Directory has an algorithm that automatically finds matching vacancies. This algorithm is similar to the one used by single persons and career networks, which first ask you to fill out a questionnaire with many keywords to tick or fields of activity to select. The open questions are also searched for keywords. While answering the open questions, stored keywords are automatically displayed and further keywords are proposed that can be selected. As soon as users confirm their input, the keywords are linked. Thus, while writing, one learns into which categories one is sorted by the text. At the end, you have to pick out at least 10 keywords that fit you and 10 that don't from a list that is generated by the keywords from the open questions. The keywords that do not fit are the opposites of the keywords that the algorithm automatically displays. The more often a keyword is mentioned, the higher it is displayed. Users have the option of assigning a weighting between 1 and 6 to their keywords. 1 means that the user likes, is good at or owns the keyword. 3 means that the user does not care about the keyword, is moderately proficient in it or has lent it out to be used. 6 is the opposite of 1.

13.7 Employment exchange through the Labour Directory

The database for workers who are working but willing to change and looking for work is connected to all private suppliers of digital job boards. Every company inland must publish all its vacancies on its profile in the Labour Directory. This does not apply to jobs that a company recasts with its own employees, the So-called "internal postings".

13.7.1 Job search

The Labour Directory job search is designed to show users the industries and companies that match their skills. Users can also specify companies and sectors themselves. The search results then automatically show which training and further education would be necessary and where this can be acquired.

The date search can be used to specify a date or period in which a job is being searched for. Jobseekers therefore have the option of waiting until a vacancy arises in the company of their choice and, if the company agrees, already receiving a treaty for future employment at the specified time. Jobseekers who do not want to wait will only be shown companies that currently have vacancies to be filled immediately. Jobseekers who have a notice period specify this period and are then also shown companies that have vacancies at the end of the notice period.

The radius search allows users to specify an address and a search radius in which the specified area will be searched for vacancies or job openings. Several radii can be searched at the same time if the user specifies several addresses. If the address or search radius is abroad, participating foreign digital job boards are displayed in the search results. The Ministry of Foreign Affairs obtains information via the embassies in the affected countries as to whether nationals are granted work permits there and for how long. The Ministry of Foreign Affairs reports all results to the Ministry of Labour as soon as international agreements are concluded or cancelled.

The search results always include the wages and which wages are paid in the same or comparable companies. A linker can be used to call up a map of wages so that jobseekers can calculate whether, when and where a move would be worthwhile. The search results from one or more districts and dates can be compared with each other in the search results. Tables and colour-coded maps show where working conditions such as wages, weekly hours, working hours, workers' rights, occupational safety and health, economic forms and other information about the surrounding area such as cost of living, association structures, health care and public transport connections exist in the specified area. For all differentiation criteria, the user can give his or her own rating from 1 "very important" to 6 "unimportant".

13.7.2 Automated application

In return for the obligation to advertise jobs, companies receive news as soon as users who have the qualifications required in the job advertisement report themselves as looking for work. Job seekers can send news to companies and have a programme automatically create an application. In the automatic application, an algorithm matches the data of the company and the person and uses it to formulate the cover letter. The person's data is used to formulate the CV. All personal data, memberships, educational paths with and without degrees, gainful activities and internships are inserted into the CV and testimonials are filed in the appendix. Analogue testimonials must be photographed once by the person and uploaded in the profile. Final testimonials are automatically imported from the Education Directory; employment references are stored in the digital personnel file on the profile.

If users have uploaded sounds, images and videos to their profile, an application video can be created automatically. Users can hide, add or rearrange content in the application and application video.

13.7.3 Satisfaction at work

The aim of all the surveys in the Labour Directory is that the amount of data should make it possible to find the perfect job for everyone. The task of the Ministry of Labour is to ensure that all workers in the country are satisfied with their jobs, receive sufficient wages to support themselves and have enough free time to relax and innovate. Through a satisfied labour force, the efficiency of the companies should increase, the people should become richer and invest their wealth in the country. This will make the country a more attractive location for companies.

14 Enterprise policy

Specific enterprise policy is the responsibility of the ministries of economy. The Ministry of Labour is responsible for general enterprise policy, which affects all companies of all economic forms. Compliance with the requirements is checked by the auditors of the Company Auditing Agency.

14.1 Holidays[105]

All companies can close on public holidays as long as the basic supply of the country is guaranteed. Persons who have to work on public holidays are entitled to one extra day off. All workers must have one day off per week. The seventh of July is a bank holiday.

14.2 Occupational safety and health[106]

Occupational safety and occupational health are promoted by the Company Auditing Agency making and explaining requirements in its audits, which have been prepared by the Institute of Occupational Health in voting with the Minister of Labour. This includes at least accident prevention with the appointment of safety officers in each company and the conclusion of accident insurance for employees. Where products are produced or used, they must be inspected for product safety by Company Auditing Agency technical auditors, especially if they involve mechanical equipment, physical agents such as loads, chemicals or biological products. Workplaces must be safe enough so that workers can spend their working lives there without suffering damage to their health.

---

105 §228,3,4 Labour: BV Art. 110
106 §215.5 Gainful employment §228.5 Work: KV Art.39, §235.4
Health and accident insurance

14.3 Environmental protection[107]

Environmental protection must be observed by all companies. Entrepreneurs may only pollute the environment in such a way that their ability to renew and their availability remain guaranteed. This requirement can be achieved either by using natural renewability, because only biodegradable substances are used, or by using human disposal and treatment processes to achieve biodegradability. The companies bear the costs of disposal.

14.4 Circular economy[108]

The companies are obliged to recycle raw materials and to adapt the production processes to the disposal processes. This includes making goods durable and easily repairable so that they can also be resold second-hand. Services are to be repeated or repaired less frequently due to their professional and qualitative execution.

14.5 Packaging

All packaging must be made of material that can decompose in the wild within 15 months. The packaging must usually bear certain instructions for consumers. These labels must also be biodegradable within the same period of time.
To introduce the processes for the new packaging materials, the ministries of innovation, education and labour are developing materials and tools for processing together with the packaging industry and the waste disposal industry.

14.6 Certificates against negative externalities

The Ministry of Labour, in voting with the departments of the Company Auditing Agency, issues limited chargeable entitlement certificates, So-called certificates, to affected entrepreneurs to internalise their negative externalities.

107 §190,1,2 Environmental protection: KV Art.31
108 §190.9 Environmental protection: KV Art.32

The certificates are related to affected enterprises and certain negative externalities and are issued by the Ministry of Labour to companies identified in the Company Auditing Agency's audit as generating negative externalities.

14.6.1 Costs of the certificates

The certificates cost so much that, on the one hand, they reflect the costs that the external effect causes for the state or the citizens. On the other hand, they should also reflect the costs that would be necessary to permanently remedy the external effect. The Company Auditing Agency's economic auditors determine the unit costs to humans and nature to undo the damage caused by the external effect, compensate victims and repair environmental damage. The Company Auditing Agency's purchasing department determines the costs that would be necessary to avoid the external effect in the future. Both costs together, plus the Company Auditing Agency's processing costs and a profit mark-up of 10% of the total amount for the treasury, result in the total amount that must be purchased in certificates. The price of certificates is tiered and the same for all certificate classes. Each negative external effect corresponds to one certificate class.

14.6.2 Purpose of the revenues

The revenues are disbursed to the payers accordingly. Victims are compensated, areas are rehabilitated or renaturalised, all involved departments of the Company Auditing Agency are remunerated and the costs for future prevention are saved in the account of the Ministry of Labour.

As soon as the amount saved by a company is sufficient to eliminate the external effect in the future, the company must implement the measure and receives the savings amount in return. In this way, certificates are supposed to make negative externalities unprofitable, ensure that they disappear and no longer occur in the long term.

The principle of simplicity assumes that harmful processes must be stopped as quickly as possible. Any increase in complexity would only create exceptions and incentives to make the harmful process less harmful. However, in order to protect the citizens, politicians and the state are obliged to prevent damage to the people as quickly as possible.

14.6.3 Example calculation

For example, carbon dioxide is a certificate class. Entrepreneurs who emit CO_2 or whose products do so must purchase a corresponding number of certificates. Filling stations would thus have to purchase as many CO_2 certificates per litre of petrol as the simple combustion of a litre of petrol produces. The principle of simplicity applies. Which engines convert the petrol into how many grammes of CO_2 is irrelevant. The Institute determines the value in its own tests.

For example, a company pollutes the air with its chimney. The Company Auditing Agency's technical auditors measure the emission of gases and the amount per second. The company is obliged to buy 12 certificates per year. Payment can be made monthly or annually. A certificate for 10 kilogrammes of exhaust gases would cost 1000 euros. This pays for tree planting (2000€), respiratory treatment (2000€ as a grant to the General Health Insurance[109]), profit mark-up (1200€), Company Auditing Agency costs (1800€) and reserves for a new filter system (5000€). Since a new filter system costs 5000€ in this example, the price of the certificate is reduced until all other costs are paid. The Company Auditing Agency's costs for a flue gas measurement are incurred for each audit until the filter system is installed, in this example only once. As soon as enough trees have been planted to be able to filter the measured amount out of the air again from 6 months before the cut-off date of the recognition of the external effect, the environmental allowance does not apply. As soon as the treatment costs of the calculated cases of illness caused by the exhaust gases have been paid, the price is reduced to zero and the company no longer has to buy certificates. The profit

109 Ministry of Health - 5.12.2 General Health Insurance

surcharge decreases proportionally to the falling price.

14.7 Business development

The Ministry of Labour's enterprise policy aims to promote the domestic economy. It accompanies the change through increasing automation in the world of work and the accompanying build-up of an Unconditional Basic Income[110] through the taxation of automated labour. The goal of full employment despite increasing automation is to be maintained by increasingly replacing timed gainful employment with research-based employment opportunities.

The reputation of domestic companies and their products is strengthened by audited quality standards of the Company Auditing Agency. Different economic forms with their own business cycles and currencies prevent all companies in the country from being involved in a downturn of the global economy. Support for research by the ministries of education and innovation enables companies to reduce research costs and bring innovations to market faster. The taxation of sales or profits makes it possible to tax human and machine labour equally and to be able to use the business tax to finance an Unconditional Basic Income in the long term. Good conditions for education, training, research, family, leisure and job satisfaction will prevent the necessarily brain drain abroad and strengthen location security. Democratic procedures between the government, entrepreneurs and employees increase the satisfaction of all participants through suggestions for improvement, compromise and pride in joint returns.

14.7.1 Unconditional Basic Income

Unconditional Basic Income is financed by business taxes from all economic forms and machine fees. The disbursement amount increases with automation. The Ministry of

---

110 Ministry of Finance - 6 Unconditional Basic Income

Finance is responsible for management and disbursement.[111] Unconditional Basic Income strengthens purchasing power despite increasing automation.

14.7.2 Digitalisation of work processes

The Ministry of Labour ensures that orders and invoices are administered digitally through its requirements for conducting business. The Ministry of Digital Affairs provides the necessary hardware, software and intranet as a digital location for notarised data traffic. Most of the digitalisation of workers' processes is handled through the Labour Directory.

14.7.2.1 Receipts

All goods and services sold must be receipted with a real or digital receipt. All goods and services are listed sorted by economic form. Each real receipt also has a barcode on it. This barcode can be photographed with your People's Computer and the taxes paid will be transferred to the account for own taxes[112] . Receipts must always be issued twice for cash payments. One copy is given to the customer, the other remains with the company and must be given to the tax auditors at the upcoming Company Auditing Agency audit. The tax auditors check the cash receipts of the companies and thereby automatically check whether cash receipts are missing that customers have scanned with their People's Computer. Those who pay cashless with a card or their identity card will have the digital receipt sent to their People's Computer and not issued in real terms.

Receipts are issued via screens at the counter. At the request of the customer, a printed receipt must be issued. By photographing the barcode on the receipt, the transaction is digitised and reported to the tax auditors. Companies must report all sales by sending the digital receipt to the tax auditors. Customers can do this, but they do not have to. For

111 Ministry of Finance - 6 Unconditional Basic Income
112 Ministry of Digital Affairs - 15.2 Tax game

cash payments, the cash registers automatically create a digital receipt for the company, the tax auditors and the customers, regardless of whether it was additionally spent in real terms or not.

14.7.2.2 Single data entry

If data such as order numbers, names, prices are used and entered digitally in a work step, re-entry should be avoided in order to save these work steps. For this purpose, the work process is digitised in such a way that copying becomes unnecessary; instead, barcodes are scanned or files are copied and pasted. This serves to increase the efficiency of the national economy, is audited by the Company Auditing Agency and enables the Company Auditing Agency to work digitally. In addition, all data and programmes are collected so that they can be fed into the Algoracle .[113]

14.8 Key industries

Domestic companies that occupy key industries and are to be sold to foreign investors or entrepreneurs at more than 50% or become insolvent may be regulated or bought by the Ministry of Labour.

Through regularisation, sales to foreigners can be prohibited. If no domestic citizens can be found as buyers, the Ministry of Labour buys the company and runs it as a state enterprise. A sale may only take place after the purchase price has been earned and only at a higher price.

The Ministry of Labour determines which companies belong to the key industries. Key industries are all companies that provide goods and services that remain necessary for the construction and maintenance of modern society in the future. These can be utilities, such as electricity, water or communication networks, which the population needs to survive, as well as new technologies that are necessary to provide many products, such as robots, and companies that

---

113 Ministry of Digital Affairs - 15.3 Algoracle

are world leaders in their field.

14.9 Insolvency

As soon as a company becomes insolvent and the Ministry of Labour asserts its prerogative to wind it up, the previously responsible Ministry of Economy is stripped of its responsibility. The Ministry of Labour is allowed to nationalise the affected companies and thus take over the management. Nationalisation of a company means that all the company's assets, including buildings and subsoil, become the property of the Ministry of Labour and former owners receive compensation equal to the residual value of the company minus any outstanding payments to creditors, employees or providers. Upon nationalisation, the Company Auditing Agency's economic auditors determine the residual value of the company, i.e. the value for cash, property, buildings and land. Company Auditing Agency business consultants run the company until the Ministry of Labour decides on a form of liquidation. The legality auditors check whether the former owners are being prosecuted under criminal law and whether their private assets can also be used to pay off debts.

As a general rule, nationalised companies are not allowed to make a loss. What exactly happens to an insolvent company after nationalisation is decided by the Minister of Labour in voting with the local affected citizens of the municipalities and, if nationally affected, with the people in a committee. The following options are proposed at the committee.

14.9.1 Transfer of ownership to the employees

The company is transferred to its employees. All employees receive a share certificate and thus have equal voting rights in the management of the company. The Company Auditing Agency's business consultants train the employees until they can take over the management of the company themselves. Then the employees elect their managers. Only when the company is sold do the employees have to pay for their share certificate.

During nationalisation, the Company Auditing Agency determines the residual value of the company, i.e. the value for cash and material resources, buildings and land. This amount is divided by the number of share certificates issued and results in the price that the employees have to transfer to the Ministry of Labour. Employees can find out the current value of the company in any audit report issued by the Company Auditing Agency. If the employees decide to sell the company, they must pay for the residual value and are paid the difference between the residual value and the sale value on a pro rata basis.

14.9.2 Conversion into a state-owned enterprise

The Ministry of Labour can open a new state enterprise or a People's Innovation Company in the premises of the nationalised company. Depending on the situation and qualifications, the workers of the nationalised company may continue to work there or be dismissed. If only other more innovative products are produced in the company, many employees may stay. If, however, a ministry has a need for the location and work equipment and plans to move existing institutions there or open a new institution there, employees must have the appropriate qualifications. If workers wish to acquire the qualifications to continue working there, the position will only be filled by another worker until the training is completed.

14.9.3 Sale to the Social Market Economy

The Ministry of Labour sells the nationalised company on the following conditions. The company may only be continued in the Social Market Economy. The citizens in a catchment area of 25 kilometres vote in favour of the sale. The company can recover its operating costs after a Company Auditing Agency consultation and audit. The proceeds of the sale cover all costs incurred by the Ministry of Labour, plus a profit margin of

10%. The majority of the employees do not want to buy the company.

The sale can be split if individual employees wish to buy shares and a buyer takes over the remaining amount. In this case, the company must become a Social Market Economy joint-stock company.

14.9.4 Rental and auction of the individual parts

The Ministry of Labour sells the nationalised company in individual parts and rents or sells the buildings to entrepreneurs or residents. The Company Auditing Agency sets the prices for the individual parts. The price is considered the starting bid for an upward auction (English auction). Any individual parts that do not find buyers in this way are sold with the price as the starting bid in a downward auction (Dutch auction). If the price drops to zero, these items are donated to the Social Villages. Items that the Social Villages or voluntary citizens do not want are disposed of. If disposal costs are incurred, the proceeds from the auctions are used for this purpose.

If buildings cannot be rented or sold, they become public domain and are freely available. Buildings that are in danger of collapse must be renovated by the users or are demolished by the Ministry of Infrastructure[114] . The vacant space remains common property until it can be sold or rented.

As a general rule, all profits made in the territory of the nationalised company must pay a 10% share of the profits in addition to taxes until all costs incurred by the Ministry of Labour have been paid.

15 Antitrust Agency[115]

The Antitrust Agency determines all economically criminal offences and punishes violations. In voting with the Minister of Labour, antitrust law, corporate law and the law against unfair competition are formulated and put to a vote of the people. The Antitrust Agency restricts economic freedom in order

---

114 Ministry of Infrastructure - 5.8 Construction Team
115 §210.4 Principles of economic order: BV Art. 94, §214 Competition policy: BV Art. 96

to ensure fair operation in all economic forms. Competition does not take place in all economic forms, but only in the market economy. The Antitrust Agency monitors all criminal offences, which the ministries of economy designate as such by law. Corporate group law regulates which acquisitions of other companies individual entrepreneurs may make in order to grow into corporations. The Antitrust Agency audits whether the resulting increase in market power could become a monopoly or oligopoly. If necessary, it can prohibit the merger or acquisition of companies to form dominant corporations.

The Antitrust Agency conducts test purchases, overt and covert investigations to uncover unfair competition, price-fixing, information asymmetries or negative externalities.

Unfair competition means that companies advertise different prices than they actually charge at the checkout. Customers should report such a case to the police immediately and wait without reporting the facts to the company until the police arrive to document the event and secure evidence. The police will forward any case to the Antitrust Agency to prosecute systematic fraud.

Price fixing means that companies agree on their purchase and sales prices in order to offer higher prices or lower quantities. The Antitrust Agency can allow customers to agree on the price at which they are willing to buy a product.

Information asymmetries mean that companies give their customers less or different information about a good or service and make profits from the information advantage. The Antitrust Agency can use coercive searches to obtain, document and publish all of a company's information.

Negative externalities mean that companies do not include all the costs caused by their goods or services in the purchase price. As a result, these costs are incurred by the environment or third parties. The Antitrust Agency has the auditors of the Company Auditing Agency examine the cost accounting of the entrepreneur and investigate whether the environment or third parties are burdened by consumption or disposal. The Antitrust Agency can order compensation payments and force the companies to adjust their prices accordingly.

15.1 Sanctions

The Antitrust Agency can impose monetary fines on all criminal entrepreneurs. The fines always consist of immediate payments and annual instalments to be deducted from profits. It can impose sentences that lead to the nationalisation or closure of the company. For foreign companies, the same applies to all assets, factories and branches located inland. In addition, the affected foreign company is prohibited from ever participating in the domestic economy again, even under a different name or under different ownership.

16 Employee protection[116]

As soon as a company has employees and not only the entrepreneurs themselves are the labourers, employee protection applies. Employee protection is mainly regulated by the ministries of economy. Only when employees need general regularisations for their activities in several economic forms does the Ministry of Labour take legislative action. The Ministry of Labour is responsible for worker protection legislation that affects all economic forms.

The requirements for entrepreneurs on occupational safety and health also apply to their employees accordingly and are regularly audited by the Company Auditing Agency's auditors for health and technology. If employees handle goods that can be dangerous to humans and nature, a licence must be obtained for devices and regular training and certification of knowledge must take place for the handling of dangerous goods. Certification of knowledge is asked for in part of the Company Auditing Agency's questionnaire to employees.

16.1 Employment contract

Employment contracts can be concluded orally or in writing. After 2 weeks, employers must provide employees with a written employment contract, which employees can reject or amend in consultation with the employer. An employment contract must specify at least the following conditions: the job

116 §228,1a,1b Labour: BV Art. 110

description, place of work, working from home, remuneration of at least 10 euros per hour, a maximum working time of 72 hours per week, compensatory time or payment of overtime, the beginning and end of the employment relationship with or without notice, whereby after 3 years in the company the employment relationship must become permanent, a notice period of at least 2 months, the duration of the probationary period of a maximum of 6 months and procedures in the event of illness. If a collective labour agreement, collective agreement or corresponding law applies, this law takes precedence over the employment contract. This is the So-called principle of subordination. However, the favourability principle also applies, which means that the employment contract can always contain better agreements than those in the law or collective labour agreement. Collective agreements can override the favourability principle if equal treatment is to be achieved.

There is a right to equal treatment in labour law. According to this, workers who have the same qualification and task should not be treated unequally. Such allegations can be made in the Company Auditing Agency's questionnaires, whereupon the auditors examine all affected employment contracts.

16.2 Organisation of working time

Working hours must be arranged in such a way that employees may work a maximum of 14 hours per day and then return to work after 10 hours at the earliest. After 6 days, work must be interrupted for 24 hours. The companies are free to organise flexitime, part-time, partner work or working from home. In the Social Market Economy, employees have a right to such working time models.

16.3 Partnering at the workplace

Workers who fall in love at work and wish to enter into a relationship must not be prevented from doing so. They must be given the opportunity to engage in partner work in the event of pregnancy after birth, if their qualifications are suitable.

16.4 Partner work[117]

Partners with or without children, but with similar qualifications, can fill a job together and take turns working. Companies decide on the basis of the qualifications of both applicants whether they are both suitable for the job. When the partners take turns at work and how, they agree with their employer. The partner work does not necessarily have to be done by life partners, it can also be friends or flatmates. What is crucial is that they spend enough time together to exchange information about their work and keep up to date so that they can continue working directly when they switch. Partners do not have to be limited to two persons; there can be more than one partner sharing a job. If there are more than two partners, several jobs can also be filled by several partners. The only decisive factor is that there are more persons than jobs.

16.5 Fun at work

Every worker has the right to have fun at work. This does not have to be the case permanently, but at least 2 times a month for 60 minutes the workforce must get the opportunity to have fun. There are many possibilities. Employees can make proposals on how to increase the fun factor in their work. Provided that it does not damage the operational process and does not disturb industrial peace, it should be introduced. Measures are permissible that promote fun for individual employees and measures that promote fun for employees working together. For example, this may be listening to music or dancing ring-around-the-rosy. What exactly this should be is determined by the employees themselves in a democratic voting.

---

117 §228.7 Labour: KV Art.39

16.6 Labour Court

If an employer or employee does not comply with the requirements of the law or collective agreements or with the agreements in the employment contract, the opposing party can have the accusation clarified before the labour court. To do so, the plaintiff must file the complaint at the local Municipal Court. Actions directly against a law are heard by the Remit Courts for Labour. Actions directed against a constitutional article are heard by the Constitutional Court.

16.7 Industrial action[118]

If employees feel unfairly treated by the state or employers, they can unify to seek improvements on their behalf. Employees can unify in their company and form a works council. They can unite in their industry and form a labour union. Employers can unite in industries and form employers' associations. The works council can negotiate with management and the labour union with the employers' association. If disputes cannot be resolved, strikes and company blockades can occur. If the basic supply of the population is threatened, strikes and company blockades can be banned by the Ministry of Labour for certain occupational groups. For each strike or company blockade banned, the company must grant all employees an additional day of paid leave as a sentence. As security of supply can be guaranteed under normal circumstances by the various economic forms, industrial action is only prohibited in acute emergencies affecting the entire population.

In principle, employees have the right to take industrial action. The ministries of economy can enact collective bargaining legislation to avert costly consequences. In the democratic management of Planned Economy and Social Market Economy, industrial action is preempted by equal co-determination. In the Social Market Economy there is collective bargaining and collective bargaining partners. If they cannot reach an agreement, a collective bargaining committee

---

118§28 Freedom of association: BV Art.28, §228,1d,2,6 Labour: BV Art. 110, KV Art.39

is set up in which decisions are taken democratically and all participants have equal voting rights.[119]
In the democratic governance of Planned Economy, the employers are the directly elected deputy ministers of all ministries and the employees are all residents of the Social Village. The employer can be deselected and its decisions can be negotiated in a committee through the veto quorum[120]. Industrial action does not make sense because if the will of the people is not respected, much harsher measures take effect for politicians than those provided for in industrial action.[121] Experimental Enterprises and Innovation Enterprises are democratically run entrepreneurial communities. There are therefore no employers and employees.

In the Free Market Economy, industrial action is current practice unless other agreements can prevent it.[122] In the Barter Economy, barter is negotiated, the municipality forms a consortium and projects carried out in a group form an entrepreneurial community. Employers and employees can choose any form of industrial action that is possible in the other economic forms.

Peace agreements in industrial disputes are called collective labour agreements. They must be agreed by a majority of the bargaining partners and then registered in the collective bargaining register. In the Collective Bargaining Register, the Ministry of Labour keeps all collective labour agreements and uses the current requirements as audit criteria when auditing the Company Auditing Agency. If there are very different terms and conditions in the same occupational group between economic forms or companies in an economic form, the Ministry of Labour can declare certain labour agreements to be generally binding. This allows the labour contract of one economic form or company to become a collective labour agreement for all companies of one economic form or for all economic forms.

---

119 Ministry of Social Market Economy - 8.4 Collective bargaining
120 Ministry of State Organisation - 9.5.14 Veto quorum
121 Ministry of State Organisation - 12.5 Punitive measures for politicians
122 Ministry of Free Market Economy - 7.3.1 Industrial action

16.8 Democratic collective bargaining

The premises of municipal and national councils are also used to negotiate collective labour agreements. Employers' associations sit opposite workers' associations there. Collective bargaining takes place at the national and municipal levels, depending on the size of the company or industry, and only when the economic form provides for collective bargaining or employees unify for it. Collective bargaining is broadcast on government television.[123] Video conferencing on the intranet between all participants is also possible. All domestic employers and employees can participate in decision-making via the intranet. Affected entrepreneurs and employees have double voting rights. Collective bargaining in the Barter Economy and Free Market Economy can be democratic and public, but it does not have to be, as in the Planned Economy and Social Market Economy. In the Planned Economy and Social Market Economy, all employers and employees must elect their own representatives.

16.9 Manager bonuses

In all companies run by managers, bonus payments must also be supplemented by malus payments. In addition to the salary payments to managers, part of their salary depends on how well the company has performed under their leadership. In this context, profits and employee satisfaction are crucial. Only if more turnover, profits or lower costs have been generated can a payout be made. How high this payout is, is decided by the employees.

As a general rule, bonuses are distributed to one account per manager. The manager can withdraw a maximum of 50% immediately. The rest flows into the company's malus fund for loss purposes. Thus, in the event of a loss, the shrinkage of turnover, profits or the increase in costs can be compensated, at least partially, from this malus fund. Malus is determined in the reverse calculation, like the payment of bonuses. When the manager leaves the company, he receives his paid-in earnings

123 Ministry of Media Affairs - 7.2.3.5 Solution Finder

from the malus fund 5 years later, if his management decisions have not generated losses in the meantime.

16.10 Temporary work

Temporary work is permitted in order to be able to react flexibly to peaks in orders. Temporary workers earn 10% more or the same as permanent employees. If they earn the same amount, a bonus is paid. The bonus is paid equally to all temporary agency workers. The bonus is equal to 50% of the profits generated by the increase in turnover. The additional earnings are intended to compensate the temporary workers for having to familiarise themselves with different teams again and again and for having to travel to the workplace differently. For the same work and the same working hours, an agency worker must receive the same pay as a company worker in the same position. Temporary work agencies must add their agency fees to their wages and must not reduce the wages of their agency workers and claim them for themselves.

Details are determined by the Minister of Labour in voting with the Ministers of Economy, unless the employees and employers' associations can negotiate it in collective labour agreements. Temporary agency workers have their own questionnaires in the Company Auditing Agency audit to determine whether the above wage regulations are being complied with.

16.11 Guest work

Guest work is only permitted in companies in the Social Market Economy and Free Market Economy. Foreigners working inland are considered guest workers and are subject to the laws of the ministries for Social Market Economy[124] and Free Market Economy[125] . Their employment contracts can only be open-ended if they are successfully naturalised and automatically terminate once naturalised persons status is

---

124 Ministry of Social Market Economy - 15.5 Guest work
125 Ministry of Free Market Economy - 12.2 Guest work

lost. Guest work is prohibited in the Planned Economy and Barter Economy. Guest workers looking for work must find suitable companies through the internet version of the Labour Directory and be invited by these companies for an interview. With an invitation from a domestic company in the Social Market Economy or Free Market Economy, guest workers receive a visa for 10 days at the embassy of the Ministry of Foreign Affairs located in their country of origin. So they do not have to leave the country to get their visa, but already have it with them on their departure.

Guest workers must report to Customs on entry and are issued with an identity card[126] and a tax account with the People's Bank to pay value added tax on cash withdrawals.[127]

When guest workers are inland, they are registered and looked after by the Ministry of Integration until they have to leave the country again. As soon as employment contracts for guest workers expire, the guest workers must leave the country no later than 10 days after that. Those who do not leave the country again by the deadline commit a criminal offence, are put on the wanted list and placed in detention pending deportation until the deportation costs incurred by the affected state authorities are paid by the guest worker or dealt with in detention. After that, they are deported. The period of detention can be shortened by allowing the costs to be paid in part by those obliged to leave the country.

As the Ministry of Labour ensures full employment in the country, the total number of domestic guest workers can be restricted. Priority is given to domestic graduates and job seekers if they apply for the same job. Guest work is primarily used to admit guests to the country, who leave as soon as learners leave the educational institutions with the appropriate qualifications and apply for all vacancies. Vacancies then include suitable positions that are currently filled by guest workers. The Ministry of Labour has the right to terminate these employment contracts after a 3-month termination period due to domestic demand.

---

126 Ministry of Integration - 4.4.1.4 Guest identity card, 4.4.1.5 Foreign citizen identity card
127 Ministry of Finance - 5.5 Tax Account

Employees who come from other European countries and whose countries are in an international union with their Ministries of Labour can take entitlements from social security, sickness and pension insurance with them when they move. The affected ministries of the member states make more detailed agreements on this in a law similar to the Employee Posting Act.[128]

In the medium term, guest work will only take place between the continents; in the long term, it will be eliminated in the unified states of the world. The Ministry of Labour, together with the ministries of economy, is dismantling all laws on guest work and only the supervision by the Ministry of Integration will remain, so that newcomers can settle in their new homeland.

17 Consumer protection[129]

To protect consumers, the Ministry of Labour enacts laws and provides benefits. The laws on consumer protection provide rights for consumers and derived obligations for the companies. The Company Auditing Agency and independent consumer organisations can sue for these rights and compel companies to take action. If consumers and entrepreneurs cannot reach an agreement, conciliation and court procedures are available. In addition, the Ministry of Labour is taking its own measures, such as the Consumer Directory and consumer information standards. The aim is to avoid information asymmetries and to enable consumers to compare prices and services before they buy an offer. If they have already bought an offer, consumers can complain about defective services and are compensated for this.

17.1 Consumer organisations

Consumers can join together in consumer organisations to jointly enforce their rights. To take action against unfair competition, they have the same rights as professional and

---

128 http://www.gesetze-im-internet.de/aentg_2009/
129 §224 Protection of consumers: BV Art. 97

business associations. If companies violate fair competition, this always affects other companies and consumers. Allegations of unfair competition can be sent to the Antitrust Agency or the Company Auditing Agency. The legality auditors investigate the cases and punish violations in order to enforce consumer law. If cases have to be heard first because companies have objected, mediation or court proceedings are conducted.

17.2 Arbitration procedure

The arbitration process is led by the Company Auditing Agency and is similar to a company committee, except that representatives of consumer organisations and affected citizens are also present. It serves the purpose of consumer protection under civil law. Conciliations can be requested in order to avoid court proceedings. They must be conducted instead of court proceedings if the amount in dispute is less than 100,000 euros. The fees for conciliation proceedings are 500 euros per plaintiff and defendant.

17.3 Affected citizens

Citizens who are affected as consumers by a product or measure of a company and suffer damage can turn to the Ministry of Labour. To lend weight to their demands, they can submit petitions and initiatives and start a quorum. Once the quorum is met, legislative proposals can be formulated in committees and responsible politicians can be appointed or questioned.

17.4 Consumer research by the Company Auditing Agency

The Company Auditing Agency conducts consumer research by collecting data on consumer behaviour. Data collection is carried out by the auditors, the Consumer Directory and by research institutions or companies participating in consumer research projects. Research includes product safety testing and deficiencies by the technical auditors, health auditors and innovation auditors. This includes consumer products in particular. Demand research includes the examination of sales figures, returns, recalls and complaints by the economic auditors. This includes special consumer groups. The data is evaluated to inform consumers and to simulate market situations. Research projects conducted in cooperation with the Ministry of Education and private institutes are coordinated by the Company Auditing Agency's Research Officer.

17.5 Cooperation with ministries

Consumer policy in the areas of energy and transport is done in cooperation with the Ministry of Infrastructure and the auditors of the Company Auditing Agency for Health and Technology. In the area of financial services, the ministries of economics and finance work with the auditors of economics and taxation. In international consumer affairs, the ministries of security and foreigners work with the legality auditors. Sustainability is developed and reviewed by the Ministry of Health in cooperation with the auditors for health, technology and legality.

17.6 Consumer Directory

The Consumer Directory serves to enable consumers to inform themselves digitally, to advise each other, to assemble, to contact responsible bodies and to report high-quality or low-quality goods and services. Through the Consumer Directory, citizens can shape their own consumer policy. The various contributions and comments for or against a product contribute to consumer education. Companies must comply with the consumer information law and are obliged to transfer their goods and services from the Labour Directory to the Consumer Directory and to provide public information on enquiries.

Every product, i.e. every good and service, must be listed in the Labour Directory in the company's profile. These products automatically receive a profile in the Consumer Directory. The profile contains all the manufacturer's details and test reports on the product. Consumers can rate and comment on the product and individual descriptions. The companies have a reply option. Posts on the profile's noticeboard can be made by consumers, the Company Auditing Agency and the company. Consumers of the same product can form groups. Suppliers of similar products can also form groups.

All Company Auditing Agency audited standards are described on the product's profile in the Consumer Directory. If customers discover a product that does not live up to its promise, breaks unusually quickly, or looks or smells improperly treated, they can report it in the Consumer Directory.

As soon as 10 consumers report a similar deficiency in a service, the Company Auditing Agency's legality auditors start their investigative work. Other clients of the service are interviewed. Legality auditors may covertly film the defective service during their undercover investigation to gather evidence.

Once 10 consumers report the same defect, all 10 consumers are asked to send the goods to the Company Auditing Agency for laboratory testing. The economic auditors of the affected economic form and the technical auditors are responsible for the testing. To do this, the consumer must call up the profile of the product in the Consumer Directory. If he ticks the field "Examination in the laboratory necessary" there, the appropriate address is automatically displayed to him, including all packaging instructions. The Company Auditing Agency will cover the costs of packaging and shipping for the consumer and will invoice the affected company for the costs of packaging, shipping and testing. If standards have not been met, the goods are handed over to the legality auditors as evidence. If a violation is found, court proceedings are opened against the company, from which criminal law[130] consequences and compensation payments to injured consumers may follow.

---

130 Ministry of Justice - 8.1.3 Corporate criminal law

17.7 Consumer information standards

All goods and services from the different economic forms can have different standards. The Ministry of Labour also sets standards that inform consumers as fully as possible so that they can exchange and unify. The Ministry of Labour, through the Company Auditing Agency, is responsible for introducing seals, certificates and labels that guarantee and regularly check compliance with certain standards. These labels must be visibly presented to customers either on the product or at the point of sale. This should make it easier for consumers to compare prices and services.

17.7.1 Price display

If similar products are not sold digitally, the products with the highest prices should be presented at the top and those with the lowest prices at the bottom. For digital sales, this setting must be preset, but can be adjusted by the user.
Prices must be indicated in at least one currency of the country. In the Barter Economy and Planned Economy localities, prices shall be indicated in the local currencies. In the Social Market Economy and Free Market Economy, prices must be indicated in the national and international currency. Prices must always also be indicated in the currency of the economic form or country in which the product was manufactured. If an international currency, such as the euro, applies in the country, this price shall also be indicated. Prices per metre, gram, litre or similar appropriate units of measurement are also indicated to help consumers compare prices and products.

17.7.2 Food traffic light

Food is labelled with a traffic light. Consumers can see how much they should consume via a pie chart, because the pieces in red, yellow or green can dominate the circle. The pie chart shows the proportions of saturated fats, non-complex carbohydrates and simple sugars in red. Unsaturated fats, complex carbohydrates and the non-degradable vitamins E,

D, K and A are shown in yellow. Protein, fibre, minerals, water and other vitamins are shown in green. If you eat more green and yellow foods, you are eating healthier. In order to be able to control the amount of calories required, the nutritional value of the product in kilocalories per 100 grams is shown above the traffic light diagram for unpacked goods and, for packaged goods, the calorie value of the entire packaged goods or per piece is also shown.

A nutritional table must be provided on the packaging or at the point of sale of the food, showing all nutrients, such as complex and non-complex carbohydrates, saturated, unsaturated and polyunsaturated fats, protein, fibre, minerals, water, degradable and non-degradable vitamins, each per 100 grams, per portion in grams and as a percentage of the recommended daily intake for a human with a requirement of 2000 kilocalories per day.

17.7.2.1 Self-control

By scanning the barcode on the product with the People's Computer, one gets to the profile page of the product in the Consumer Directory. Here, further information is displayed and it is possible to create a nutrition plan, which is more or less detailed, via the personal data on the intranet. The Ministry of Health offers a calorie calculator with which the personal calorie requirement per day can be calculated. For this, users have to enter their age, body weight, height, gender, sleep per night in hours, activity level in daily activity, type of sport and intensity of training per week in hours.

If the personal data is kept up to date, barcodes of the products taken and the approximate amount of the product consumed are indicated as a percentage, the body weight and muscle mass can be controlled by the consumers themselves and implemented in a diet plan as desired.

17.7.2.2 Test criteria

The decisive factor for the traffic light is the composition of the ingredients in the product. The traffic light is based on the list of ingredients, but the manufacturers must inform the Company Auditing Agency of the exact amount of ingredients when inspecting the goods.

The Company Auditing Agency's health auditors check all foodstuffs and categorise them. The composition of the raw materials for the human body is recorded. The raw materials are carbohydrates, protein, fat, minerals, vitamins and fibre. The individual raw materials are broken down further if necessary.

Carbohydrates can be complex. This means the body needs longer to break them down so it can consume them. This keeps you fuller for longer, keeps blood sugar levels constant and prevents cravings. Examples of this are wholemeal flour instead of white flour. With white flour, the grains are first hulled before they are milled. Fibre and minerals are lost. Fructose, also called multiple sugars or fructose, is similarly sweet, but must first be converted into human sugar, So-called simple sugar or glucose. When consumed in excess, the body converts carbohydrates into fat and stores it in fat deposits.

Fats can contain saturated, unsaturated or polyunsaturated fatty acids. Saturated fatty acids are similar to human fatty acids, raise cholesterol levels and end up in fat deposits if consumed in excess.

Vitamins E, D, K and A are considered non-degradable and accumulate in the body when consumed in excess and can then cause health problems under certain circumstances.

Such effects of differently produced or compounded foods are researched, evaluated and included in Company Auditing Agency audits by the health auditors together with the Institutes for Evaluation and Environmental Medicine .[131]

All foods are checked for their health safety. Ingredients that are harmful to one's own health or to the environment when consumed in excess are sorted into the red category. If legal limits are exceeded, the food or other goods are banned, taken out of trade and recalled if necessary.

131 Ministry of Health - 4.5.4 Institute of Environmental Health

The health auditors and citizens, through the Ministry of Health, can have limits set in laws if the necessary majorities are reached. The health auditors must agree with a majority of 75% and citizens with 30%.

17.7.3 Origin display

The notification of origin is checked and issued by the legality auditors. If necessary, enquiries about foreign companies are requested through the staff of the embassy there. Undercover investigations during enquiries by legality auditors are permitted. All products are subject to mandatory labelling as to where and by which company they were processed and manufactured in whole or in part. Where possible, labelling shall be on the product or at the point of sale. If the product originates from more than one country or economic form, the places, forms and names shall be presented in a table showing the percentage where what part of the product was made.

Further data can be accessed via the Consumer Directory, for example what standards apply in the economic form or country and how high the wages and cost of living are for the workers. By photographing the barcode on the product with the People's Computer, the profile page of the product in the Consumer Directory is automatically called up.

17.7.4 Seal of approval

The seal of quality is awarded by the economic auditors for Social Market Economy. Products of the Social Market Economy receive the protected quality seal "Quality made in [name of country]" because in this economic form the strictest requirements for environmental protection, occupational safety and health, labour rights and technically extensive quality checks are carried out on the product as well as on the company management. The quality seal is affixed to the product or at the point of sale.

17.7.5 Environmental traffic light

A traffic light function reveals how environmentally friendly the product, including packaging and shipping, is in production, trade, consumption and disposal. The traffic light is developed and awarded by the health and technical auditors.

Green means environmentally friendly, i.e. in all parts only environmentally compatible waste, exhaust gases or waste water are produced. Environmentally compatible means that the product can be disposed of untreated in the open air without causing damage to humans or nature and that it will biodegrade after a maximum of 2 years. Humans and nature enjoy rights that the product does not cause them unannounced costs and irreparable damage. If costs and damage do occur, the company is liable for them.

Yellow means in all or some parts non-environmentally sound waste, exhaust or effluent is produced, but can be fully treated to be biodegradable. Humans and nature do not enjoy rights in some countries of production of the product that the product does not cause them undue costs and irreparable damage. If they do, the company is not fully liable for this.

Red means that all or some parts produce non-environmentally safe waste, exhaust or effluent that cannot be treated, recycled or made biodegradable. Humans and nature do not enjoy rights in most countries of production of the product that the product will not cause them undue costs and irreparable damage. If they do, the company is not liable for it.

"Red" products can be banned by law from production, import, export and possession by the Ministry of Health. Foreign products that are marked as "planned to break" in the Consumer Directory and have also been inspected by the Company Auditing Agency are automatically marked red. Domestic products that break according to plan, i.e. products that break after a certain time or frequency of use, will be banned and the company will be taken to court. If found guilty, affected consumers are compensated and the company is sentenced under corporate criminal law.

18 Finance economy

The finance economy consists of all companies that work with money and assets. The ministries of economy issue their own laws on opportunities for the finance economy. General laws that apply to all financial businesses are issued by the Ministry of Labour.

The Ministry of Labour issues securities legislation in cooperation with the ministries of economy. This regulates who may issue securities where and what conditions apply to owners. Securities are shares, bonds and betting slips.

The Ministry of Labour supervises the finance economy on the Social Market Economy and Free Market Economy stock exchanges. The Planned Economy and Barter Economy do not have stock exchanges, but residents of the Barter Economy can invest their savings on the People's Stock Exchange. Residents of the Barter Economy can invest on the People's Stock Exchange and the stock exchanges of the Free Market Economy. The People's Stock Exchange is reserved for domestic companies and nationals. The only exception is domestic funds.[132] Social Market Economy companies may only issue shares and bonds on the People's Stock Exchange. Domestic companies in the Free Market Economy may only produce inland in order to be allowed to issue shares or bonds on the People's Stock Exchange as well.

The domestic stock exchanges are the People's Stock Exchange[133], Ideas Stock Exchange[134] and the stock exchanges[135] of the Free Market Economy with their stock exchanges in certain cities.

In addition to investing money in shares in companies (shares) and loans to companies or states (bonds), the finance economy also includes financial market betting (certificates and derivatives) and other money games (betting and gambling).

---

132 Ministry of Finance - 11.11.3 Domestic funds
133 Ministry of Finance - 11.8 People's Stock Exchange
134 Ministry of Finance - 11.9 Ideas Stock Exchange, Ministry of Innovation - 9.11.1 Ideas Stock Exchange
135 Ministry of Free Market Economy - 10.3 Stock exchanges

18.1 Money games[136]

Money games are offers by companies in which persons wager money and bet on the outcome of a certain event. They include, for example, slot machines, sports betting, games of skill, casino games and the trade of certificates and derivatives on stock exchanges. These may be real or digital gaming venues. At all gaming venues, information on contact addresses for the treatment of gambling addiction must be visible to gamblers at all times.

Any company offering such gambling services must obtain a casino licence from the Ministry of Labour. The levy for the concession is based on the revenue of the casino and may not exceed 80% of the gross gaming revenue. The levy is used to cover the costs of the Ministry of Labour and to transfer a sufficient share to the Addictive drugs Health Insurance[137] in voting with the Ministry of Health. The share is based on the treatments provided in the health system for gambling addiction. Casinos are audited by the Company Auditing Agency to ensure that they comply with the requirements.

18.2 Joint-stock companies[138]

The Ministry of Labour regulates the basic conditions for joint-stock companies in the Companies Act. Furthermore, the ministries of economy may issue additional regularisations. Free Market Economy, Social Market Economy and Planned Economy joint-stock companies must comply with principles that can ensure sustainable corporate governance in the interests of investors. Companies that cannot disclose the names of their shareholders will not be eligible to participate in the domestic economy. The Company Auditing Agency's legality auditors check that all requirements are met and report any violations. In the event of a final conviction, a fine of up to 6 years' remuneration or an imprisonment of up to 3 years will be imposed. If dividends on shares are remitted abroad, tariffs will be charged at the value added tax rate.

136 §222 Money games: BV Art. 106
137 Ministry of Health - 5.12.3 Addictive drugs Health Insurance
138 §216 joint-stock companies: BV Art. 95

18.2.1 General meeting

All shareholders meet annually in real and digital form at a general meeting. There, an election of persons takes place for the leader and all other members of the board of directors, all members of the remuneration committee and a proxy vote.

Shareholders can lend out their vote to elected proxies. Financial companies that hold shares because they have launched funds vote in the interest of their clients and must limit and disclose their voting and any other influence on the general meeting.

Voting and debates at the general meeting are conducted equally in real and digital form. All shareholders are entitled to vote, whether they are at the general meeting or voting remotely by electronic means. Voting shall involve the employees of the joint-stock company. In the Free Market Economy, their votes are for information purposes only, for shareholders to be informed independently of the board of directors and management. In the Social Market Economy, employees have the same voting rights as any shareholder who owns a share, unless they themselves own additional shares. In the Planned Economy, only employees are entitled to own shares in their joint-stock company.

The management of a joint-stock company is the responsibility of all shareholders, who are represented between general meetings by the board of directors and primarily by the chairman of the board. Labour unions can buy shares through their membership fees to enable employees to participate.

18.2.1.1 Statutes of the general meeting

The general meeting determines in the articles of association how much money the members of the board of directors, the executive board and the advisory board may spend on their business activities, how much debt they may incur or how much of the company's assets they may lend, and how high their pensions are for retirement provisions. The articles of association must also specify strategies for the success of the joint-stock company, or what investments are envisaged in ventures with states or other companies, and how profitable existing investments are. The articles of association specify how many mandates and employment contracts the members of the board of directors and the executive board may have outside the joint-stock company and the term of their employment contract with the joint-stock company.

18.2.2 Board of directors

The chairman of the board of directors has the same rights as all other members of the board of directors and assumes organisational tasks, but has the casting vote in voting because the number of board members must be odd. The board of directors is responsible for the management of the joint-stock company and can appoint a management board and an advisory board, but it cannot relinquish responsibility.

18.2.3 Remuneration Committee

The remuneration committee consists of staff from the human resources department and the personnel board. It submits proposals to the general meeting for the remuneration of the President and all members of the board of directors, the executive board and the advisory board. The shareholders are free in their voting and may, but are not obliged to, follow the proposals of the remuneration committee.

Members of the board of directors, executive management and advisory board members do not receive any remuneration other than that paid to the general meeting. Remuneration in advance, compensation, premiums for the purchase and sale of companies or employment contracts for advice or activity in a joint-stock company are not permitted.

18.3 Financial Supervisory Authority[139]

The Financial Supervisory Authority is an agency similar to the Antitrust Agency. Its president is a directly elected politician. Together with the Minister of Labour, it formulates the uniform rules for the financial markets of the Social Market Economy and Free Market Economy and puts them to a vote of the people. All requirements of the Financial Supervisory Authority are checked by the auditors of the Company Auditing Agency for economy and legality. All audit data of the Company Auditing Agency may be used for this purpose. The Financial Supervisory Authority brings together the regularisation of all companies that deal exclusively in money and assets. These are namely banks, stock exchanges, insurance companies and companies that offer money games.

The Financial Supervisory Authority is responsible for ensuring that financial companies are solvent, incorruptible and sustainable, without encouraging bankruptcies and favouritism. It is also responsible for ensuring that consumers of financial products have the same information as the suppliers.

Citizens can petition[140] the Financial Supervisory Authority and its responsible President. Consumers can turn to the Financial Supervisory Authority with complaints at any time. They do not incur any costs as a result. They will receive information on the progress of their complaint as soon as the responsible body has vindicated itself or as soon as any preliminary investigation arising from the complaint has been concluded. In order to facilitate and safeguard investment advice for consumers, all financial companies must be included in the financial market register for banks, investment advisors, stock exchanges, securities dealers, insurance companies and insurance brokers.

Through its mechanisms, it ensures domestic financial stability in cooperation with the ministries of finance, digital affairs, foreign affairs, justice and security. With the Ministry of Finance, People's Bank and Note-issuing Banks are used

---

139§160.4 Financial Supervisory Authority   : KV Art.105, 106, §217.4 Banking and Insurance: BV Art. 98, §222,2 Money games: BV Art. 106
140Ministry of State Organisation - 9.10.11.6 Petition

to ensure the solvency of the state and price stability. The Ministry of Digital Affairs contributes through the testing, production, deletion and simulation of digital financial technologies, payments and cryptocurrencies. The Ministry of Foreign Affairs ensures the international fight against money laundering, war financing and economic crime through its embassies and intergovernmental agreements. The Ministry of Justice ensures legal certainty with its investigations and verdicts. The ministries of justice and security ensure that sentences are enforced with their law enforcement agencies.

18.3.1 Banking Supervisory Authority

The Banking Supervisory Authority formulates the Banking Act in voting with the Minister of Labour and puts it to a vote of the people.[141] In it, banks are obliged to share all account data of their customers with the Banking Supervisory Authority in order to combat money laundering. The data accesses are entered in the Access Directory[142] of the persons affected after the conclusion of the Investigation and Court proceedings and at the latest after their termination or expiry. The banks themselves are reviewed when they are established and during their ongoing operations. This includes the minimum capital requirements to hold sufficient own funds and to be able to guarantee solvency on time. The Banking Supervisory Authority can set the deadlines if payment delays occur. In addition to sufficient capital, investments must not only be made in risky investment opportunities, but a broadly diversified risk should secure the entire asset portfolio of a bank. Risk hedging through derivatives and certificates is only permitted for banks in the Free Market Economy. Banks in other economic forms must select lower-risk asset classes, such as bonds, precious metals, real estate and shares in Social Market Economy companies. If investments are made by banks through algorithms or management systems, the source codes are checked for legality by the Ministry of Digital Affairs.

---

141 https://www.gesetze-im-internet.de/kredwg/index.
html#BJNR008810961BJNE013306123
142 Ministry of Digital Affairs - 7.5 Access Directory

The necessary data is collected by the technical auditors in the course of the regular audit. In the area of risk control, risky financial transactions must be covered with sufficient capital without causing insolvency in the event of a loss.

Banks must apply for a banking licence when they are incorporated. The application results in an initial examination by the Company Auditing Agency. If banks violate the requirements of the Financial Supervisory Authority, the legality auditors can enforce written warnings, monetary fines and the revocation of the banking licence.

If a bank does become insolvent, the insolvency procedure is applied. In the Free Market Economy, the bank's customers bear all losses equally; only the state enjoys preferential rights in the realisation of the residual value for outstanding taxes or fees. In the Social Market Economy, the outage insurance bears the losses and fully compensates all investors. People's Bank is also subject to the Financial Supervisory Authority, but receives its terms of business through laws of the Ministry of Finance.

18.3.2 Insurance Supervisory Authority

The Insurance Supervisory Authority formulates the Insurance Supervision Act in voting with the Minister of Labour and puts it to a vote of the people.[143] In it, the insurance companies are obliged to fulfil the requirements of the Banking Supervisory Authority as far as possible and only to make adjustments to the business model. The decisive factor is that sufficient security assets are available to guarantee the fulfilment of the concluded treaties.

18.3.3 Exchange Commission

The Exchange Commission for the People's Stock Exchange, Ideas Stock Exchange and the free exchanges is the Ministry of Labour. The ministry cooperates in supervision with the Ministries of Innovation, Finance, Social Market Economy

---

143https://www.gesetze-im-internet.de/vag_2016/

and Free Market Economy. It controls the access authorisations of the exchange traders and their market transactions. The exchanges are operated and trades are settled in accordance with the requirements from the affected ministries of business or innovation, which is regularly audited by the Company Auditing Agency. The Exchange Commission monitors compliance with the rules at the time of listing and trading. The Exchange Commission has the right to temporarily or permanently ban the trade on one or more stock exchanges in the country as well as the trade of one or more securities. The ban on trading must be justified by the protection of the country's economy or the rule of law and can be assessed in court on a case-by-case basis.

In the case of trade in securities, the Exchange Commission formulates the Securities Trading Act in voting with the Minister of Labour and puts it to a vote of the people.[144] Securities can be shares, bonds, derivatives or certificates.

Stock exchanges are obliged to report any suspicion of insider trading, price and market price manipulation. In addition, banks and stock exchanges are required to share with the Exchange Commission the names of buyers and sellers of securities, the price paid and all reports of affected listed companies. The retrieval for law enforcement purposes including the names will be displayed in the Access Directory of affected citizens once the process is completed. The data retrieval for simulation purposes of the Algoracle will be anonymised without names and does not need to be reported via the Access Directory.

In order to monitor market transparency, all sales prospectuses in which securities are described for customers are reviewed by the Company Auditing Agency. The review includes the correctness of the form and content as well as the solvency of the issuer of a security.

In order to check fair competition and anti-trust law, takeovers of majority shareholdings can be regulated or prohibited. This includes in particular the influence of financial companies, such as pension funds and their asset management companies. If, for example, ten asset managers each own 10% of the shares

---

144https://www.gesetze-im-internet.de/wphg/index.html

of companies in an industry, the asset managers constitute an oligopoly. If the asset managers themselves are joint-stock companies and their shareholders are only the other nine asset managers, an unlawful monopoly results. Domestic unlawful monopolies or oligopolies are broken up by the Antitrust Agency. Foreigner unlawful monopolies or oligopolies are excluded from economic activity inland. The Ministry of Free Market Economy may issue exemptions for its economic form for domestic and foreign asset management companies in the law.

18.4 Rating agency

The rating agency is an autonomous fee-funded not-for-profit agency of the Ministry of Labour with its own President, who is a directly elected politician. It is entitled to access all data from the Company Auditing Agency, the Antitrust Agency and the Financial Supervisory Authority in order to check solvency (creditworthiness). Solvency must be checked whenever financial products such as shares, bonds or derivatives of companies or government bonds are sold.

The rating agency is paid by the creditors because the rating saves them extensive investigation. The amount is added to the purchase price of a share, bond or other financial product that is based on the rating agency's rating. When selling for the first time, the So-called issue, the customer can still withdraw from the purchase until the rating has been prepared and published for 7 days.

The Company Auditing Agency's audits have to be paid for by the companies and the state and carried out on a regular basis. Therefore, ratings of companies and state agencies located in the country are the most favourable because much of the rating service has already been provided by the Company Auditing Agency.

The rating agency can set further assessment criteria. It must publish all its rating criteria so that the people can influence them via the veto quorum. It is subject to regular, unannounced audits by Company Auditing Agency legality auditors and ongoing monitoring by economic auditors. Economic auditors must also give a rating on the creditworthiness of companies, the state and its municipalities whenever the CAA is commissioned to do the rating. If the ratings differ, the presidents of the Company Auditing Agency and the rating agency must justify themselves to the people and the Minister of Labour. Unlawful ratings may result in criminal proceedings for fraud. The rating agency takes on the task of avoiding adverse selection. Adverse selection occurs when debtors and creditors are differently informed and it makes sense for the debtor to present himself better in order to obtain more favourable credit conditions.

The rating agency assesses the solvency and the risk of default on payment with the probabilities on a scale of 1 to 9. 1 means the highest credit rating with a negligible risk of default in the long term. 2 means that the long term is more difficult to assess. 3 means that unforeseen events affecting the overall economy or industry increase the default risk. 4 means that defaults can be expected if the overall economy deteriorates. 5 means that defaults are to be expected even if the industry deteriorates. 6 means that defaults are likely if the economy is bad. 7 means that no defaults are to be expected only in the event of favourable developments. 8 means that the company or the state is already in delay of payment. 9 means a partial or complete default on payment.

Only financial products with a risk rating between 1 and 3 are admitted to trading on the People's Stock Exchange. If they fall below this, they are excluded from trading.

18.5 Stock market readiness

The Company Auditing Agency checks the stock exchange readiness through its data. This is done automatically by an algorithm that searches all internet pages relevant to the stock exchange, all necessary directories of the intranet and all data of all audits of the Company Auditing Agency. In detail, these are the internal company data and numbers, an industry, product and competition analysis, a peer group comparison in terms of size and activity with comparable companies already listed, the current stock market environment, trends and ratings by analysts and banks as well as a determination of the current value of the company. No minimum value is prescribed, nor is there a minimum size. It is only crucial that the company is not indebted and has a corporate strategy to generate profits in the long term. Growth in the value of the company or profits is not prescribed.

The entrepreneurs can apply to the Company Auditing Agency for an initial public offering or the economic auditors recognise in the initial public offering the opportunity to make the company more efficient and propose the initial public offering to the entrepreneurs. If entrepreneurs wish to have an initial public offering and the algorithm does not consider the company to be ready for the stock exchange, advice is given as to what would have to happen for the company to be ready for the stock exchange. The algorithm outputs all the anonymised data that, in its digital investigation, argued against the company being ready for the stock exchange. Companies can work through this list and be newly examined.

If the company is ready to go public, the economic auditors of the Company Auditing Agency conduct a strengths, weaknesses, opportunities and threats analysis with the owners and employees of the company.[145] If the analysis speaks in favour of an initial public offering, the Company Auditing Agency passes on the approval for an initial public offering to the Exchange Commission. If a regular audit by the Company Auditing Agency reveals that the conditions for IPO readiness are no longer met, the deficiencies are noted in the audit report and a deadline is set for its rectification. For consumer protection, deficiencies and deadlines are reported to the CAA. If the deficiencies are not remedied within the time limit, the Exchange Commission withdraws the right of the state or company to trade on the stock exchange.

18.6 Stock exchange trading

Different rules and laws apply to trade on the various stock exchanges, which are determined by the respective operators of the exchanges. Domestic citizens who are joint-stock

145https://de.wikipedia.org/wiki/SWOT-Analyse

companies may only issue registered shares. If shares are sold, the new buyers report their name to the company. The company sends this information to the Company Auditing Agency when it is audited. The Company Auditing Agency reports to the Ministry of Labour if the majority shareholders are abroad.

18.6.1 Share prices

Each share has three share prices. Through the three prices, savers can quickly see whether a price increase is exaggerated or justified. Depending on whether the three prices are far apart or close together, the price is exaggerated or justified.

First, this is the company's equivalent value per share, which the Company Auditing Agency announces after each audit. The value of a joint-stock company is divided equally into many shares. If the value of the company increases, the initial share price increases and the company is allowed to issue more shares equivalent to its growth. If the value of a company falls, the share price falls and shares may be bought back.

Second, this is the price of the past 3 sales of a share in a company. If the selling price of the share increased between the last 3 consecutive sales, the second price increases. If the selling price fell, the second price falls.

The third share price is the last sale price. This is the current price of shares on the international stock exchanges to date.

18.6.2 Change of stock exchange or economic form

If a joint-stock company in the Free Market Economy wants to change to the Social Market Economy, it must comply with other rules. This may require share splits and buybacks so that the company can issue enough shares to all its employees and there are no more foreigners shareholders. Switching from the People's Stock Exchange to an international stock exchange is possible as long as its terms and conditions are adhered to. Switching from an international exchange to the People's Stock Exchange is only possible for domestic companies whose shareholders are exclusively nationals.

19 Agriculture[146]

The Ministry of Labour, in voting with the Ministry of Health, sets common standards for the agricultural and forestry companies of the various economic forms. Agricultural and forestry law is designed to ensure the supply of healthy food to the population and to prevent famine, including for individual humans inland, as well as to protect and care for the environment and landscape so that meadows, forests, rivers, lakes and seas can maintain their protective, useful and welfare functions. Particular attention is paid to the equitable distribution of agricultural and forestry land between economic forms. Each economic form must first be able to satisfy its local basic food demand. After that, national food demand must be satisfied. Only if there is a surplus of food and renewable raw materials without the state having to spend tax money on agriculture may food and renewable raw materials be exported.

19.1 Agriculture in the economic forms[147]

The farmers and foresters of the Barter Economy pay attention to the renewable management of forest and arable land. To ensure that they receive sufficient yields for house building and catering despite the strict nature conservation regulations of the Barter Economy, the Company Auditing Agency supports them with a free initial consultation.

The Free Market Economy's farmers and foresters can use the latest technology, guest workers and international investors to increase their yields as much as they like and make any offers they want as long as they do not damage humans and nature. The farmers of Planned Economy cultivate the gardens and fields and care for the paths and parks of the Social Villages. They secure these natural livelihoods in cooperation with the residents and amateur gardeners.

146§220,1a,1f Agriculture: BV Art. 104, KV Art.51
147§220,1b,1c,2 Agriculture: BV Art. 104, KV Art.51

The farmers of the Social Market Economy can take on tasks for the Ministry of Infrastructure and care for the landscape. They receive direct payments for this.

The Ministry of Labour can grant an interest-free loan to peasant companies in the Barter Economy, Planned Economy and Social Market Economy if they are no longer able to help themselves. The loan is always connected to an audit and advice from the Company Auditing Agency.

19.2 Crop failure insurance[148]

In the event of damage caused by natural disasters, such as droughts, storms, fire, floods, disease or pest infestation, the Ministry of Labour offers crop failure insurance. The insurance is Tax-funded for all companies in the Planned Economy and Social Market Economy. Companies in the Barter Economy and Free Market Economy can purchase it for a fee. The crop failure insurance replaces the lost income from the cultivation and breeding of animals and plants in the event of damage with cash or non-cash benefits.

Member contributions are used to help the Ministry of Infrastructure build water pipes and catchment tanks in vulnerable zones to reduce the damage from natural disasters. Contributions from policyholders are used for the regularisation of damage. If this is not enough, disaster bonds are issued on the People's Stock Exchange, the maturity of which depends on how long it takes agriculture to recover from a disaster.

19.3 User communities[149]

Farmers and foresters in the Social Market Economy and Planned Economy can join together to form user associations, So-called cooperatives. In these cooperatives, they can jointly buy more at a lower price or jointly purchase and use modern inputs. They are also entitled to use the Procurement Office

---

148 §220.3a Agriculture: BV Art. 104
149 §220.1d Agriculture: KV Art.51

and the Purchasing Department of the Company Auditing Agency. This state service is remunerated with a cost-covering surcharge plus 10% profits on the price.

19.4 Company Auditing Agency audits in agriculture[150]

In the Company Auditing Agency audit, farmers are offered opportunities for advice, training and research available in educational institutions. New research results are sent by the institutes and colleges to the Ministry of Labour so that innovation auditors can pass them on to suitable farmer-owned companies.

Through its audits and advice, the Company Auditing Agency promotes nature-based management practices through research, exchange forums for successful strategies and evaluation of ongoing success models. The innovation auditors specialise in creating agricultural ecosystems that benefit and protect each other. They check the location in question in terms of soil conditions and weather patterns. By using a drone, the data is automatically collected and a model is calculated, which makes it clear whether there is room for improvement. This is done by automatically comparing the data with the Innovation Database and the Success Model Directory. The agriculture companies receive the automatic results in their audit report. If the measures are to be implemented by the Company Auditing Agency, advice must be booked.

The Ministry of Labour issues regulations for food labelling so that consumers know the origin, quality, production method and processing methods. In cooperation with the Ministry of Health, safe and dubious places of origin, qualities, ingredients, production methods and processing methods are identified, recorded, verified and, if necessary, corrected by the health auditors of the Company Auditing Agency.

The Company Auditing Agency's health auditors determine whether conservation measures are necessary on the farmer's land. In particular, the use of medicines, fertilisers, chemicals, genetic modifications and other potentially hazardous

---

150§220,3f,1e,3d,3e,4 Agriculture: BV Art. 104, KV Art.51, BV Art. 197

adjuvants are categorised into risk classes by the Ministry of Health, controlled by the Company Auditing Agency and regulated by the Ministry of Labour. These non-natural substances may only be used indoors with appropriate filters, hygiene measures, barrier and purification systems for exhaust gases, wastewater and waste. In particular, genetically modified seeds, pollen, plants and animals must be screened so that they cannot enter the environment. Health auditors take regular samples around the genetically engineered agriculture facilities.

19.5 Food quality

The Ministry of Health pursues the quality policy for food. The Ministry of Labour ensures implementation in the food industry. Food should be healthy and thus free of harmful additives. Healthy food can become unhealthy if too much is consumed. Therefore, citizens should be able to obtain comprehensive information about their food. Manufacturers of food are obliged to draw up a list of ingredients with all compositions, quantities and prices of all ingredients, which the health auditors obtain and check in the same way as the finished food in the trade. The health auditors produce an ingredient list, nutritional table and food traffic light for the food in their inspection report. During the regular inspection, the method of cultivation or animal husbandry and the location are recorded and also listed in the inspection report. Every supplier of a food must provide this information from the test report to the consumer before the purchase in order to comply with the consumer information law. Animal products and killed animals that may pose a risk must first be examined by veterinarians before they can be placed on the trade. This is the case, for example, with trichinae in meat.

The food industry will be obliged not to add any addictive substances to food, such as simple sugars, salt, glutamate or saturated fatty acids. Exceptions are permitted if contributions are made to the Addictive drugs Health Insurance[151] . The Ministry of Health issues limits for ingredients and regulations

151 Ministry of Health - 5.12.3 Addictive drugs Health Insurance

on which foods and ready meals are healthy.

19.6 Land market[152]

In the case of a sale of the land ownership of agricultural land, the Ministry of Infrastructure uses the state's right of first refusal if this can strengthen the farmer's land ownership through a lease-purchase procedure. The sale of agricultural land to foreigners is prohibited. Renting is only permitted if there is no demand by domestic farmers.

Farming companies that care for land owned by the state without being able to generate income from it receive direct payments in return. The Company Auditing Agency audits the agreed care of the land.

19.7 Mineral resources[153]

The Ministry of Planned Economy is responsible for the administration of mineral resources in the country, and the Ministry of Infrastructure for mining. After a subsidiarity vote[154] , administration can be transferred to one or all municipalities. Groundwater and mineral resources above and below ground within the national and maritime boundaries may not be exploited by companies, but only by state enterprises which the people can control through politicians.[155]

19.8 Food industry

The food industry includes all companies that deal with food. In detail, these are gardeners, farmers, the processing industry, wholesalers, retailers and mail-order companies, as well as the catering industry. In order to provide food on a sustainable, widespread and diverse basis, food production is carried out by private individuals, the state, permaculture farms and industrial agri-factories. In order to bring producers and consumers of

152§220,3h,3b Agriculture: BV Art. 104, 197
153§210.7 Principles of economic order, §220.5 Agriculture
154Ministry of State Organisation - 10.3 Subsidiarity vote
155Ministry of Planned Economy - 11.1.10 Mineral Resources

food together as far as possible without intermediaries, the Labour Directory offers producers the opportunity to offer goods by mail order and to set up standing orders. For this purpose, the profiles from the Labour Directory and Food Directory can be connected.

19.8.1 Animal products

Animals intended for consumption must be kept in a species-appropriate manner so as to have little stress. Their exhaust gases and waste must either be neutralised by their surrounding ecosystem or collected, converted to electricity and processed. At the time of their death, they must have no diseases and their death must be as short and painless as possible without agony. Feed shall not be contaminated with poisons or polluted by contaminants. Feed should consist mainly of nutritious algae and aquatic plants grown in the ocean so as not to consume land for animal feed. Medicines that are also suitable for humans and can produce resistant pathogens must not be used on animals. Only indoors with special shielding is the rearing of genetically modified animals allowed.

19.8.2 Plant products

Plants intended for consumption must be kept species-appropriate and free of fertilisers, pesticides and pests. Monocultures are to be avoided in the environment, alternating tall vegetation and deadwood are to protect against drought. Irrigation is only allowed as close to the roots as possible. Indoors, monocultures and the use of fertilisers are permitted until 2 weeks before harvest. Genetically modified plant products are only allowed indoors with special screening.

19.8.3 Sustainability

The food industry makes its contribution to sustainability in the handling of animals and plants in the ecosystem.

Sustainability is considered to have been achieved when animals and plants are kept in a species-appropriate manner and live in a circular economy, and when humans and all future generations can be adequately supported with affordable and healthy food. Therefore, only the production of seed with seed-resistant varieties is permitted. Seed-proof varieties are capable of forming seeds themselves, which can be sown.

19.8.4 Climate protection

To protect the climate, permaculture increasingly uses more field areas year-round and increases their vegetation per cubic metre. Perennial use increases yields and the filtering effect for CO_2 and the conversion effect of toxins. In addition to permaculture, indoor agriculture also ensures that CO_2 is extracted from the air drawn in.

19.8.5 Generation security despite climate impacts

In order to be able to guarantee production security despite climate impacts, the food industry is broadly positioned. To ensure sufficient yields despite storms, drought, heat and cold, food is produced on outdoor surfaces and indoors. The outdoor areas are designed to store a lot of water and to protect against solar radiation and cold by growing vegetation at different heights. Heat traps serve as storage for water and heat. The dense year-round vegetation protects fields and forests from storms and forest fires. Permaculture on outdoor areas thus contributes to improving the climate and to production security.

The agribusiness is exclusively for indoor use and can therefore be used anywhere. It requires little water because irrigation happens in a targeted manner and the water is treated for each other in a circuit by filters, plants and fish. In addition to this protection against drought, the building above or below ground protects against cold, heat, fire and storms. The electricity for the agribusiness must be generated from renewable energy sources.

The Ministry of Labour, together with the Ministry of Security, develops measures to ensure food security for various disaster situations and puts them to a vote of the people.

19.8.6 Conventional and organic agriculture

Conventional agriculture will be banned as soon as permaculture has grown sufficiently. On all land used for conventional agriculture, subsidies will only be paid for the switch to permaculture. As soon as permaculture without subsidies produces the same yields as conventional agriculture with subsidies before, the subsidies will be stopped.

For this changeover, the area of the conventionally farmed farmers is recorded and divided. The current yield in tonnes per hectare is determined and an area for the first permaculture field is calculated. Since permaculture yields more,[156] than conventional agriculture, the farmer can continue to practise conventional agriculture on the remaining field until his permaculture field has reached the initial yield under entirely conventional agriculture. On the remaining conventionally used fields, farmers may now practise organic agriculture or also plant permaculture fields.

For organic agriculture, as with conventional agriculture, subsidies are discontinued as soon as a sufficient yield is achieved through permaculture. Since even organic agriculture does not come close to permaculture yields, its products are significantly more expensive.

19.8.7 Near-natural agriculture: Permaculture

Permaculture is the deliberate establishment and arrangement of perennial crops and livestock so that all living things perform tasks for each other so that the ecosystem grows and thrives stably. This eliminates the need for bought-in pesticides, fertilisers and irrigation, and the yield grows with the plants and animals from year to year.

156https://www.deutschlandfunknova.de/beitrag/landwirtschaft-mehr-ertrag-und-umweltschutz-durch-permakultur?token=upox8g0mggpgysk mjlxtvgve8etoevqi

Permaculture knows how to create small, stable ecosystems that are optimally adapted to the environment in order to make it as useful as possible. The establishment of non-edible or poisonous plants serves to introduce nutrients into the soil, to bring water to the surface or to eliminate pests. Usually edible plants also serve these purposes, but non-edible or poisonous plants often also have a medicinal effect and are therefore planted. Ponds are created to store water and heat and to concentrate sunlight in a heat trap. Plant varieties from warmer regions can then be planted in the heat trap. Tall trees are planted to provide shade. The constant goal is to choose the type and location of living organisms in such a way that they fulfil as many tasks as possible, apart from being eaten. In this way, the living organisms save the farmer and forester labour time and costs and automatically increase their yields to their natural maximum growth point.

Just as permaculture adapts to the environment, agriculture machinery must also adapt to permaculture. Digital technology is used to power machines for harvesting and care. They can distinguish between plant varieties, test the degree of ripeness and harvest in a species-appropriate way without damaging the plant. Agriculture research is being directed towards the invention and development of such machines.

19.8.7.1 Conversion of agricultural land[157]

The conversion of agricultural land to permaculture takes place in four steps. First, the farmers map their farmland, including soils, temperature and rainfall. For this, they receive plans from the Company Auditing Agency as to when and where which measurements are to be taken, and satellite images in which they enter the results. Secondly, these data are used to develop plans that are adapted to the respective region down to the individual square metre. The plans are used for landscaping and sowing, thereby establishing high-yield and stable ecosystems throughout the

---

157 §220.3g Agriculture: BV Art. 104

country that do not require artificial fertilisers, pesticides or irrigation. Third, agricultural robots are being developed to provide automated harvesting and care on an ongoing basis. Fourth, farmers are increasingly converting their agricultural land to permaculture until the perennial growth has doubled the amount previously produced conventionally. The remaining agricultural land is being renatured or turned into building land.

When converting to permaculture, the first years are characterised by high labour input and financial losses until the plants have grown sufficiently to provide cost-covering yields. During this time, money is paid out to the affected farmers from the Innovation Fund. The amount is determined by the auditors of the Company Auditing Agency in an audit of the minimum living costs of the farmer and his family. If the size of the farm allows, the direct payments can be reduced because cultivation is still possible on the conventionally used fields. Conventional fields are gradually converted into additional areas of permaculture every 2 years. The landscaping measures can be done by the Construction Team of the Ministry of Infrastructure.

Large permaculture farms can be fully automated with cable cars for robots and harvest baskets running through a permaculture field. On the one hand, the cableway stands on stilts that can be automatically telescoped up and down. The rope can sag more or less to get closer to the ground in individual sections. On the ground, robots run on four or more stilts so as not to compact the ground too much. Drones fly through the air and helium balloons hang from the ropeway with robotic arms for harvesting or cutting plants. An automatic chicken cage, open at the bottom and the diameter of a bed, drives onto areas to be prepared as a new bed. The cage is driven over the bed and the chickens plough it up by scratching and fertilise it with their droppings. Once the bed is prepared, the cage moves with the chickens to the next bed. If there are no beds, the cage drives faster over the paths to keep the vegetation there short. Once a day, a collection robot comes and collects the eggs from the hen house. Geese move freely on the grounds. A pig herd can be established from 2 hectares of permaculture field, and as the size increases, other farm animals such as cattle or sheep. Individual animals of different sizes can also live on the permaculture fields. On large permaculture farms, which also practise forestry and fish farming, cattle and sheep live in herds on large contiguous areas. Cattle are always used as draught animals here.

For better irrigation, small streambeds are created between the more or less large ponds of the heat traps, through which edible fish and amphibians move and are caught in fish traps.

19.8.7.2 Conversion of urban parks and paths

At least one park per city must be permaculture-oriented and offer as many varieties of nuts, legumes, fruits and vegetables as possible. Trees and shrubs planted along the path or roadside are edible or produce edible fruits.

19.8.7.3 Conversion of native gardens and allotment and small animal breeding associations

Volunteers can cultivate their gardens and balconies with permaculture. Instructions are available free of charge on the intranet or for a fee at Company Auditing Agency courses. Clubs for allotment gardeners can release plots for permaculture and enter into cooperations with neighbouring small animal breeding associations. Chickens can scratch the soil to prepare it for new beds, rabbits keep the grass short. Which varieties are planted in private permaculture is up to each individual. However, they should still match each other in order to support each other.

19.8.8 Agriculture away from nature: Indoor agribusiness

Indoor agribusiness is the use of technical means to grow food indoors under artificial conditions. There, plants grow in monocultures with nutrients precisely matched to them in hydroponics, temperature, humidity as well as strength, colour, distance and luminous duration of the light. LED technology allows lamps with the appropriate light spectrum, low power consumption and heat generation to provide sufficient lighting on every floor. Solar cells on the roof and on the façade as well as other electricity and heat generating or storing systems for domestic use provide the necessary energy. Water pipes can be used to transfer nutrients to the water, which then flows in a circuit along the roots. Evaporation through sprinkling is not necessary. The nutrients come from a water tank in which fish are kept. Their excretions serve as fertiliser.

19.8.8.1 Agri-factories

In agri-factories, plants can grow on pallets in high racks until they are ready to be harvested and placed on the harvest conveyor belt by a robot. After the pallet is harvested by machine, it is automatically replanted with the prescribed variety or can remain stocked with the same crop for another rotation. In-house biogas plants and tanks for fish farming and water treatment produce the fertiliser that is added to the water in hydroponics. Agri-factories are clean rooms into which no pests can penetrate. Bee colonies only live in the clean room for pollination and cannot leave the agri-factory. Animals can also be bred in agri-factories, as long as this is possible in a species-appropriate manner. They need additional exercise through running wheels and treadmills with video screens, places to retreat, toys and hygiene rooms where they are automatically showered and washed. Grooming robots clean the floor of excreta. Dressage robots are able to train the animals to behave in certain ways, for example to let out their excrement only in the hygiene room under running water. To create a more pleasant atmosphere for animals and plants, music is played at times in agri-factories.

19.8.8.2 Cultivation cabinets and indoor plant systems

In grow cabinets and indoor plant systems, the lighting, irrigation and hydroponics systems of large-scale industry can be used on a small scale. Private individuals can grow their own food, medicinal or intoxicating plants on a small scale.

19.8.9 Distribution

End consumers, restaurateurs, retailers and wholesalers can find available food in the Food Directory and order it online or pick it up themselves at a specified address during given opening hours.

19.8.10 Agricultural markets

The agricultural markets are composed of the suppliers in the form of hobby gardeners, gardeners and farmers with their cultivation methods of permaculture, organic agriculture and indoor agro-industry. The demanders are the consumers, hobby cooks, restaurateurs, processors, retailers and wholesalers who may specialise in different farming methods. The Ministry of Labour, through the Food Directory, provides a common market organisation between the different suppliers and demanders.

Competition law changes depending on the economic form. In the Free Market Economy, producers compete freely and do not share their production methods, quantities and prices and are not allowed to conclude agreements. In the Social Market Economy, producers share knowledge of production methods and can coordinate product ranges in the event of overproduction. In case of shortage, the Minister of Social Market Economy can demand a certain product range for Social Market Economy. In Planned Economy, food producers are organised in a cooperative, share machinery, labour, seeds, breeding animals and cultivation methods. In Barter Economy, food producers exchange food for labour and cultivate the land mainly by hand and, if necessary, with livestock and simple tools made of wood and metal in the style of permaculture. Competition arises from different strategies and resulting yields.

19.8.11 Export of agricultural products[158]

Agricultural companies that are particularly environmentally and animal friendly are granted export permits to other economic forms and countries, provided that this does not increase the price of food inland or reduce the amount of food below the basic supply.

19.9 Forest, hunting and forestry policy[159]

Municipal and national state forestry expels areas for Barter Economy Zone where residents practice agriculture and forestry. The remaining areas are planted in a natural way and with climatically adapted trees and shrubs. In the short term, bamboo will meet the demand for wood and replace steel. Bamboo can grow about 20 metres within four months in tropical summers, several times as fast as the fastest tree. Bamboo can quickly reforest forest areas destroyed by drought or storms and raise the water table. Due to its strong leaf production, it fertilises itself. The state forest is implemented according to Social Market Economy regulations. This means mixed forests with deadwood, accessible only by forest roads but without logging roads. The trees are transported to the forest road, which can be used by transporters, either by horses, horse-like machines, helium balloons or helicopters. The helium balloons carry water balance tanks that release water at the point where the tree was standing. An appropriate amount of water is released, corresponding to the weight of the felled tree. The weight of the water tank corresponds to the weight of the loadable trees. The tanker delivers the helium, fills the balloons with it at the operation site and anchors them to the ground. It then drives to the nearest hydrant and fills the tanks with water for the balloons' balance tanks until they

---

158 §220.3c Agriculture: BV Art. 104
159 §193 Forest: BV Art.77

return from their harvest.

Fire protection regulations apply in the Free Market Economy, with firebreaks to adjacent forest areas and villages. Pesticides may not be used and harvesters must be electrically powered. In Planned Economy, there is only forestry for trees that are not edible. Each Social Village creates a small patch of forest and manages it according to the requirements of the Social Market Economy, using only livestock as draught animals.

The owners of the forest areas can release their areas for hunting. The state forest areas outside the Barter Economy Zone are hunted by hunting clubs. The hunting clubs are considered as companies because they sell the hunted game or parts of it. They are obliged to pay Social Market Economy business tax on this and a further 10% is added to the tax rate as a right to use the state forest for hunting.

19.10 Fisheries policy

The majority of fish consumed in the country must come from domestic farmed in inland waters or farms. The fisheries structure is divided by fishing in public waters and breeding in designated facilities. The market for inland fish, sea fish and farmed fish is possible in all economic forms. Only Free Market Economy companies are allowed to fish only in farms and outside territorial waters. The waterways are being converted and expanded for fish farming. The facilities of the Ministry of Infrastructure for flood and drought protection as well as the pumped storage facilities for storing and generating electricity are operated with water. Fish farming will be carried out in basins suitable for this purpose in these facilities. All angling supplies must be made of material that is naturally degradable in water and on land. Anglers who nevertheless fish with material that does not decompose will be convicted of environmental pollution, as fishing lines can break off and this event can hardly be traced.[160] Fishing is not allowed where water sports are practised, because physical exercise serves health and fishing is only for recreational pleasure.

On the coast, maritime permaculture families are operated

160 Ministry of Justice - 8.6.1 Environmental pollution

under water, which may be fished as designated fishing zones with catch quotas that have a 110% renewal capacity. This should make it possible to catch more and more fish and seafood and to harvest aquatic plants. For harvesting seafood, plants and catching fish, underwater robots are on the move, which are either guided and supported by lines or carry batteries. The lines or battery charging stations are connected to power stations for waves, currents and tides in the surrounding area. International fisheries policy is overseen by the Ministries of Foreign Affairs, Health and Free Market Economy.

19.11 Knowledge management

The Ministry of Labour collects data via the Company Auditing Agency on what yields the agriculture companies had in the past year, of what kind they were able to produce and how many kilograms they were able to sell. The statistics are kept via the inspection programme and supplemented with weather data for the location. In this way, a virtual model can be created for each farm, on which soil conditions, in which weather, which animal and plant species are most productive. Through the sales data, a probability for the demand of the coming year can be created.

The Ministry of Labour gives voluntary companies the opportunity to share their information in order to find successful strategies. The auditors and advisors of the Company Auditing Agency use the data as a basis for planning in order to make recommendations on the appropriate animals and plants to breed and how much of them should be provided and when. The data can be analysed by the Algoracle and used to make recommendations and simulations for one's own entered initial situation. Planned Economy companies are obliged to share the information with everyone. Social Market Economy entrepreneurs are obliged to share the data with all Social Market Economy companies. Barter Economy and Free Market Economy companies can decide for themselves whether, how much and with whom they share data. The Company Auditing Agency accesses all data to check security of supply on an ongoing basis. If supply shortages are identified, companies can also be forced to produce certain foods for a limited period of time.

Agricultural and forestry research is conducted in collaboration between a food industry network, the ministries of labour, innovation and education. The Company Auditing Agency's innovation auditors ensure that suitable farms are linked with appropriate research institutes and chairs at the state colleges. The colleges can have large-scale field studies conducted in the farms and the farms can submit research assignments.

Through the link, gardeners, farmers and foresters can also quickly identify education and training opportunities. However, innovation auditors also suggest education or training in the audit if it could be useful for the company.

19.12 Food culture

The dietary culture is designed to support the human with the necessary nutrients, namely protein, carbohydrates, fats, fibre, vitamins and minerals. Different cultures have developed different foods to provide the nutrients. The aim here is to offer as much variety as possible and to find the best ways of preparing and composing it. Variety can be restricted in cultural protection areas to preserve a different cultural character. The best type has a gentle preparation and a balanced composition of nutrients. In order to be able to pursue a food culture that is as diverse as possible, all the necessary food should be cheap and available. The food industry takes care of this.

A sustainable diet becomes possible when the nutrients protein, carbohydrates, fat, fibre, vitamins and minerals cost as little as possible. A diet low in carbohydrates and fats but high in protein and fibre should not cost more than a reverse diet. A large inexpensive supply of fruit, vegetables and wildlife is given to the citizens through permaculture. The citizens should be given the opportunity to adhere to the guideline values for a healthy diet.[161]

Food waste is to be kept low. This is promoted firstly by throwing away less food, secondly by producing less and thirdly by feeding discarded food or turning it into biogas.

---

161 Ministry of Health - 6.1 Nutrition

Food retailers and caterers must give away and, if necessary, dispose of food when its best-before date expires. The expiry date must be determined by the Company Auditing Agency before a food is marketed for the first time and regularly checked thereafter. Before restaurants or traders are allowed to throw away food, they must first reduce the price, sell the goods to secondary retailers or give them away to employees, customers, Non-profits and Social Villages. The rubbish bins in which food is disposed of must only be closed in such a way that humans can still open them. They must be freely accessible.

A throwaway society for food is a weakness of the market economy that can be prevented by bringing suppliers and consumers so closely together that consumers inform suppliers of their desired order and the suppliers produce the goods for them. To shorten delivery times, demanders can use standing orders to instruct suppliers to regularly deliver an agreed quantity of certain foods at a certain time. Changes to the order list can be made up to a specified date. This function is supported by the Food Directory. If end consumers have a standing order with one or more farmers, they can offer a tandem service. This means that the food is delivered in a reusable container that remains with the customer and can be used as a lockable organic bin. As soon as the next delivery of goods arrives, the containers are swapped. The organic waste is used by the farmer as animal feed or converted into electricity and fertiliser in the biogas plant. This allows the farmer to see which of his products are more likely to be consumed and by whom, and to adjust the shopping basket accordingly for the next delivery with the customer's consent.

19.13 Food Directory

In the Food Directory, any food producer can create a profile. This can be farmers, agribusiness, cooks or gardeners. The profile includes an online shop, a calendar and a profile page with a noticeboard. In the profile, it is entered where which form of food production is carried out and when. For individual food products, groups are created in which all profiles of the food producers involved are automatically members. This makes the supply chain traceable for customers and producers and buyers can see what is available and when. The food producers can indicate a price, means of exchange or to give away. Those who do not produce food but own it and want to throw it away can also give it away via the Food Directory. A photo together with a description or scanning the barcode on the packaging, details of pickup and shipping are sufficient to create an entry in the category "to give away". Consumers can look for food sources through the proximity search and have the goods picked up there or shipped via the online shop. Freely available food sources on state land are also listed and can be updated by users. Standing orders and delivery contracts can also be arranged through the Food Directory. This option is available to private individuals, restaurateurs, retailers or wholesalers.

If consumers want to create a personal meal plan, they can use the Food Directory programme. In the programme, goals can be specified that are to be achieved with the diet, such as losing weight, saving money, Italian cuisine and lactose-free. This can be used to create cooking recipes and shopping lists. If consumers also specify their gender, age, height, activity level and weight, the optimal amount of nutrients can be calculated for the quantities in recipes and orders. An algorithm proposes order plans from which producers what should be ordered and when. The decisive factor in the default setting is the price and the proximity to the consumer. Consumers can set further filters, for example, settings of the environmental traffic light or food traffic light, only certain forms of agriculture or quality classes.

Seeds, cuttings or breeding animals can also be ordered in the Food Directory. Producers can add information for planting, breeding and processing to their profile and have their methods rated by users. Successful ratings are included in the Success Model Directory.

19.14 Nutrition of the future

The food of the future must be able to feed all humans in a healthy way over generations without destroying nature as the basis of life. The dynamic media democracy envisages many different cultures living in the united states of the world in the long term. Agriculture is practised differently in different areas and cultures. The aim is to find the most productive methods for each location and to share them worldwide.

19.14.1 Short term

In the short term, permaculture is gradually being imported until it provides competitive yields. Humans can increasingly harvest additional food for themselves through publicly accessible edible plants and animals. Farmers increase their revenues firstly by no longer having to buy in seeds, fertilisers, pesticides, feed and medicine. Secondly, permaculture uses perennial plants that yield more as they grow.

The technological food industry develops systems for growing plants and keeping animals indoors. The assortment ranges from showcases for the living room to multi-storey fields in high-bay warehouses with artificial lighting and irrigation systems, including fish farming for fertilisation.

Humans support themselves through subscriptions to a farmer, farm shops, mail order, supermarkets, restaurants, as well as by harvesting their own food from urban green spaces and growing it indoors or in their gardens. They are increasingly learning to understand food labels.

19.14.2 Medium term

In the medium term, permaculture will produce an oversupply of food that will also provide enough food to keep all farm animals. Once the entire food range has reached its cost-covering minimum and demand is saturated worldwide, prices will not fall any further. The lowest level of food prices is reached when this means that only the operation of harvesting robots and processing machines has to be paid for.

The Company Auditing Agency continuously calculates what price covers the costs up to the end consumer and can set this price as the minimum price. If the oversupply persists, farms can be converted into residential and holiday resorts for self-sufficiency, or the land can lie fallow and continue to grow until it becomes wild or is used again. Many independent ecosystems have emerged that are adapted to their environment and benefit more than they damage, even without care and management.

The technological food economy is expanding its capacities in old mines with factories underground until sufficient tropical crops and animals grow in colder climates and no longer need to be imported. A circular economy has emerged that meets its electricity and heat needs from heat exchangers, biogas, wind turbines and solar panels. Fish and small animals convert the plant biomass into fertiliser, and the plants turn the fertiliser into food. A technological ecosystem has been created that can be exported to other planets.

Humans support themselves by mail order directly from the producers with the basket of their election, because the prices per kilogram are approximately the same for each foodstuff by adjusting the harvest or capacity to the demand. In permaculture, more or less of each variety is harvested or left to rot in the field. In indoor production, land is used differently, because humans as a whole cannot eat more when saturation is reached. To waste as little food as possible, consumers report their orders to producers in advance if possible. These foods are the cheapest and guaranteed to be available. Those who need certain foods quickly have to reckon with higher prices or have them supported by the catering industry.

19.14.3 Long term

In the long run, permaculture on land, water and in the air has led to a purification that has reversed the pollution of the previous three centuries. The rivers and lakes are drinkable, the air quality healthy everywhere. Food now accounts for only 10% of the cost of living. Self-sufficiency is possible for all humans as long as they want to spend time harvesting. All populated areas are overgrown with plants edible to humans and populated with edible animals.

The technological food economy is capable of allowing humanity to survive indefinitely underground or on alien planets without an atmosphere. It is an integral part of disaster management. Self-sufficiency can survive vegan in their homes as long as they can generate enough electricity or have lit space.

Food trade takes place mainly between producers and consumers by mail order. Visits to the farm shop or market take place for leisure and to get to know each other. Farms offer free holidays if guests help with the year-round harvest. Surplus food is returned to producers and fed or converted into electricity in biogas plants.

Humans offer their specialities in restaurants and care for old food crafts in cultural protection areas. Anywhere in the world, any food can be produced at any time, thanks to permaculture and technological food management.

20 Company Auditing Agency[162]

The Company Auditing Agency is the largest agency of the Ministry of Labour. It is responsible for auditing all ministries, state enterprises and companies of all economic forms. It forms the empirical and economic basis of labour law.

The Company Auditing Agency is modelled on the "Technical Inspection Association" (TÜV)[163]. However, not only technology is tested, but also companies, their business figures, working conditions, goods and services. Similar to motor vehicles, companies receive test badges and test reports that show the condition in test results using standardised procedures. Deficiencies requiring inspection may consist of violations of the law or mismanagement. The Company Auditing Agency audits ministries and state enterprises annually and all other companies every 2 years.

---

162 §215.6 Gainful employment: BV Art.95
163 https://www.tuev.online/

20.1 Audit of private companies

The Company Auditing Agency's goal for citizens is to have as few and as orderly corporate failures as possible. It pursues this goal through three procedures. First, company data is collected in the audits, which can be used to simulate the national economy. Market gaps in supply and demand and future market conditions can thus be made visible in scenarios with a higher probability. Secondly, the Company Auditing Agency's contacts with all companies can ensure that success strategies are shared between companies to increase productivity. To this end, the Company Auditing Agency maintains the Success Model Directory. Third, the Company Auditing Agency can facilitate terminations for companies by finding other jobs for affected employees in cooperation with the Employment Office to maintain full employment.

The services of the Company Auditing Agency differ in the ifferent economic forms. In the Free Market Economy, all services of the Company Auditing Agency are chargeable. In the other economic forms, the services are fully or partially Tax-funded.

20.2 Audit of state agencies[164]

The Company Auditing Agency is a statutory oversight body through which citizens can exercise their superintendence over state activities. Through the audits, every state activity is recorded and made public for the electorate. In this respect, there can be no corporate secrecy for ministries and state enterprises, unless they are People's Innovation Companies. In People's Innovation Company, no facts that could jeopardise the scope of protection of a patent and monopoly position may be published.

The Company Auditing Agency supports ministries and state enterprises in quality management, sabotage protection, surveys and their evaluation, corruption prevention and disciplinary matters. Quality criteria for state services are

---

164§70, 2 Supervision: BV Art.169, §71, 4 Review of effectiveness: BV Art.170

set in detail by citizens through law and by ministers. The Company Auditing Agency is responsible for the independent verification of these criteria. It does this by evaluating the insights into the accounts, questionnaires and tests, the results of which it publishes in the audit report. Through this evaluation, acts of sabotage and corruption can be uncovered, punished and avoided in the future. The list of deficiencies in the audit report helps superiors to take disciplinary action against affected employees.

To review the effectiveness of state activities, the Company Auditing Agency sends auditors to the Surveillance Television monitoring teams[165] .

The Company Auditing Agency audits the economic activities of companies in order to be able to grow the national economy uniformly in the long term. This includes the review of tax levies and balanced or profit-oriented budget management in company accounting. The review is intended to detect corporate bankruptcies at an early stage and, if possible, to avert them. The results of the inspection are displayed to the entrepreneurs through inspection reports and data queries from the company's profile in the Labour Directory.

The Company Auditing Agency's objective for the state is to provide state services as transparently, efficiently and innovatively as possible and to avoid corruption, duplication or lack of responsibility. State services are provided within the framework of the ministry's Social Market Economy economic criteria and are audited accordingly.

When auditing ministries and state enterprises, the tax auditors proceed like the Audit Court and check whether tax money and profits have been used in accordance with the requirements of the budget vote and not wastefully or illegally. All other areas are audited in the same way as for Social Market Economy companies.

---

165 Ministry of Media - 12 Surveillance Television

20.3 Advisory service

An additional service of the Company Auditing Agency is management consultancy. Ministries, state enterprises and companies can receive advice on how to remedy deficiencies identified in the audit, use success strategies of other companies, purchase cost-effectively and jointly master internal disagreements or reforms in a direct-democratic and moderated manner.

20.4 Accountability report[166]

In order to verify its effectiveness, the Company Auditing Agency must submit an annual accountability report. This must show what revenues were generated from monetary fines and fees for examinations and advice and what the revenues were used for. In the case of company closures by the Company Auditing Agency, reasons must be published on the basis of the last audit report. In the case of monetary fines and company closures, the court judgments must also be listed. The accountability report also contains a statistical evaluation of how many establishments were audited and how many of them had no, slight or serious, many or few deficiencies.

20.5 Employees

The head of the Company Auditing Agency is a directly elected politician from the Ministry of Labour. In order to find expert auditors, experts from other ministries are brought in and temporarily work as auditors in the Company Auditing Agency. The auditors work in a team that audits together. The composition of the team always remains the same and consists of auditors for tax, health, economics, technology, innovation and legality. These six audit areas are managed in their own departments, which receive their applicable regulations in the form of laws from the respective ministries.

The Company Auditing Agency's staff consists of workers who are permanently employed by the Company Auditing Agency

---

166§71, 4 Review of effectiveness: BV Art.170

and auditors who are replaced every 5 years. The permanent staff is responsible for the administration of the Company Auditing Agency and instructs the new auditors in their areas of responsibility. The auditors come from the ministry responsible for the department. The Ministry of Education has teachers who teach and research in educational fields that cover at least one departmental area. Because teachers always have to gain work experience in companies, these qualified teachers are auditors in the Company Auditing Agency at least once in their career.

Ideally, auditors should already have professional experience in a company and a ministry. Young citizens who have just completed their initial education can also apply as auditors. Within the 5 years, they must then decide whether and in which ministry they would like to continue working in the state service afterwards.

To avoid corruption, companies do not know which employees they will be auditing in the next audit. Auditors, in turn, do not know with which auditors they will use to audit the next company. During audits, undercover investigators are brought in as auditors on a random basis to check whether other auditors are corrupt, accept bribes or perform favours. The undercover investigators are either permanent staff who also train auditors or civil police staff[167] .

20.6 Audit programme

The examination programme is installed on a device equipped like a People's Computer. It is registered as a second device to the auditor and may only be used for official purposes. The examination programme enables the auditors to work through their checklists and to access all checklists of all other auditors. To facilitate entry, the audit programme can retrieve and enter all company data stored on the intranet. Whenever laws prescribe criteria, these criteria are displayed and a link to the law is created in the Law Directory. The programme automatically records new laws and amendments in the company that make more or less laws binding on the company.

---

167 Ministry of Security - 7.5 Civili police

All audit procedures and results must be documented in the audit programme. In subsequent audits, data records can be transferred and completed. This allows the audit to be paperless and exclusively digitalised.

20.7 Departments of the Company Auditing Agency

The Company Auditing Agency maintains 7 departments. One department is responsible for management consultancy. The other 6 departments take care of the audits. All departments are coordinated by the Ministry of Labour with the responsible ministries. Examinations and advice are prepared and followed up in the departments. The departments are located in the capital cities of the respective ministries. The auditors travel around the country and evaluate their data at home.

20.7.1 Tax auditor

The tax auditors check companies to see if they pay taxes and ministries to see how they use the taxes. They report to the Ministry of Finance[168] and ensure compliance with the tax laws of the ministries of finance and economy. They cooperate with the Tax Investigation Department[169] by reporting suspicious cases and receiving investigation results. If the tax auditors suspect tax evasion, they alert the Tax Investigation Department. If the tax auditors find tax evasion, they secure evidence and open court proceedings against the participants involved and against the company itself. In court proceedings, the Tax Investigation Department takes over the investigation.

20.7.1.1 Tax audit for companies[170]

Companies are audited to determine whether they pay

---

168 Ministry of Finance - 5.7 Company Auditing Agency tax auditors
169 Ministry of Security - 8.3 Tax Investigation Department
170 §215.6 Gainful employment: BV Art. 95

sufficient taxes according to the tax rates in their economic form.

In the Free Market Economy, 20% sales tax is due. The tax auditors check the turnover through a cost-performance calculation based on the business figures and compare the payments via the tax account at People's Bank. All prices and the quantity sold are recorded and multiplied together to calculate the turnover. From this amount 10% is calculated. This amount must match all tax payments made since the last audit. If there are discrepancies, the tax auditors alert the Tax Investigation Department.

In the Social Market Economy, 30% profit tax is due. The tax auditors check the profit against the business figures by means of a revenue surplus calculation and compare the payments via the People's Bank tax account with this. All prices, the quantity sold and all costs are recorded. By calculating price times quantity minus costs, the profit is determined. From the profits, 20% is calculated. This amount must match all deductions via the People's Bank tax account that have been collected since the last audit. Any shortfall must be paid within 6 months, any surplus will be paid into the company's People's Bank account immediately after the audit. If costs exceed revenues and a loss is made, the tax auditors alert the business consultants.

In Planned Economy, 40% property tax is due. The tax auditors check the assets of the residents of the Social Villages and the asset growth. 40% is deducted from all increases in assets. This amount must agree with the payment transactions on the People's Bank account and the deductions made there via the tax account. If there are discrepancies, the tax auditors alert the Tax Investigation Department.

In the Barter Economy, 10% capital gains tax is due at the People's Bank and 20 hours per month of community work. Assets can be invested in any other economic form and are taxed according to the tax rates there. The tax auditors check the duty rosters in the town halls of the Barter Economy Zone. If too few hours have been worked, the working hours can be made up within one month. If this does not happen, the working hours must be served as imprisonment in a Ministry of Justice prison.[171]

20.7.1.2 Tax audit in ministries[172]

Ministries and their state enterprises are audited to ensure that taxpayers' money is spent as determined by the population in the budget vote.[173] The tax auditors take over the Financial Supervisory Authority of the state. All prices for services and costs are audited. If the costs turn out to be higher than agreed in the budget vote, the ministry has to pay the money from profits of its operations until the next budget vote. The responsible politician must seek approval in a committee of enquiry.[174]

If ministries receive a financial and burden equalisation[175] , as approved in the budget vote, it is audited whether, where and why the ministries or their operations spend more tax money than they receive.

20.7.1.3 Procurement Review Board

The Procurement Review Board examines all orders that citizens wish to award to companies of any economic form through voting or ministries. The Procurement Review Board is the central body for participation issues when it comes to public orders. It audits the procurement system of the State Procurement Office and the admissibility for the award of state orders to private companies.

---

171 Ministry of Justice - 7.5 Detention
172 §160 Financial Supervisory Authority: KV Art.105, 106, §158,3
Finance of Ministries: BV Art.183, §161,4 Financial and burden
equalisation: KV Art.105, 106
173 Ministry of Finance - 9.5 Budget vote
174 Ministry of State Organisation - 12.5.2 Committee of enquiry
175 Ministry of Finance - 7.1 Financial and burden sharing

20.7.2 Health auditor

The health auditors inspect companies and ministries to ensure that they comply with sufficient measures for occupational safety and health and environmental protection. They are authorised to inspect all economic and state activities that have to do with the health of humans and nature. If there is damage to the health of humans or nature, entrepreneurs, companies or ministries and ministers are arrested by the legality auditors and punished accordingly after a court verdict.[176]

Health auditors report to the Ministry of Health[177] and ensure compliance with the laws of the Ministries of Labour and Health. Employees of the health auditors are employed physicians, pharmacists and researchers of the Institutes of Occupational and Environmental Medicine of the Ministry of Health and scientists of Agriculture, Forestry and Water Management of the Ministry of Education. The annual report is published in the Environment Directory .[178]

If the health auditors find violations for the first time, they have the technical auditors check the violations to determine the proportion of technical deficiencies. They also have the infringements examined by the innovation auditors to determine the possibility of remedying the deficiencies in an innovative way. They state the results in the inspection report and set a deadline by which the deficiencies must be remedied. If violations are not remedied and deficiencies are not permanently eliminated, they report this to the legality auditors after the deadline. The legality auditors open a procedure for environmental pollution. If the health auditors find repeated violations, the legality auditors are immediately alerted to collect fines and open criminal proceedings against persons who commit repeated violations.[179]

---

176 Ministry of Justice - 8.1.3.5 Damage to humans and nature
177 Ministry of Health - 4.4 Company Auditing Agency health auditors
178 Ministry of Health - 6.6.1 Environment Directory
179 Ministry of Justice - 8.6.1 Environmental pollution

20.7.2.1 Occupational health and safety audit[180]

Companies and ministries are regularly audited to ensure that they comply with the applicable laws of occupational health and safety. They are supported in this by the Institute for Occupational Health. On the one hand, the Institute provides requirements on what a safe and healthy workplace should look like and how certain materials or machines should be handled. On the other hand, the auditors see methods and examples of use, which they document and forward to the Institute. Especially in the machinery sector, the health auditors work together with the technical auditors to share expertise and jointly assess situations as safe and healthy. This applies in particular to the chemical and biological safety of, as well as the physical effects on, equipment and operational buildings at workplaces and products.

If the auditors find deficiencies, the Institute provides the deficient companies or ministries with proposals on how to ensure a safe and healthy workplace and handling of materials and machinery. The auditors, in voting with the companies or ministries, set a date by which the deficiencies must be remedied. The latest date is the next inspection date.

All workers are obliged to report to the health auditors all occupational accidents and diseases that have occurred since the last audit. Incidents and environmental circumstances are documented by the auditors and evaluated in the laboratories of the Institute for Occupational Health in order to find prevention strategies or limit values.

Animals and plants used commercially or by the state are also subject to occupational health and safety law and must be treated accordingly by their keepers. The health auditors check that animals and plants are kept in a manner appropriate to their species.

180§228.5 Labour: KV Art.39

20.7.2.2 Environmental protection audit[181]

Companies and ministries are regularly audited to ensure that they comply with the applicable laws on consumer protection, animal welfare and plant protection, as well as on proper procurement, processing, marketing and disposal or recycling. In this process, the health auditors are supported by the Institute for Environmental Medicine. On the one hand, the Institute provides guideline values for exposure limits and expiry dates. On the other hand, the auditors provide the Institute with samples and application examples for innovative, effective or ineffective or damaging behaviour. The auditors document the processes and share them with the Institute of Environmental Medicine.

The auditors clarify whether the producers pay sufficient costs for disposal. They check the payments of the originators to the disposing companies and compare the costs of the disposers with the payments of the originators. During the audit, it is important to ensure that as many recyclable materials as possible are used in order to be able to participate in the circular economy. Non-recyclable substances are considered pollutants and must be demonstrably taken to a screened and accessible storage facility.

The decisive factor is the cost of separating waste into raw materials and pollutants, storing pollutants until they become recyclable, and converting other materials into saleable raw materials. The price of raw materials is deducted from the costs.

Through their regular audits, the auditors ensure that new innovations are constantly introduced in order to increasingly manage without finite raw materials and pollutants in a circular economy. They ensure that at all times the natural environment is so healthy that present and future generations can survive at least at the current standard of living. The consumption of raw materials is compared with their natural renewal capacity and must not exceed it. To test limits, the auditors undertake area-wide sampling of air, soil and water at different heights and depths, but especially around vulnerable facilities for the

---

181 §190 Environmental protection: KV Art.31, 36, BV Art.74, KV Art.32

production, recycling or disposal of pollutants.

20.7.3 Economic auditor[182]

The economic auditors examine companies and ministries to ensure that they comply with the applicable laws of the Ministry of Labour and their economic form. The management review follows the concept of peer review, whereby entrepreneurs and expert assessors review the economic viability of a company.

The business ratios are recorded in order to be able to better simulate the national economy. The aim is to predict company developments and make future forecasts for the economic development of all economic forms.

The examination of the constitutional principles of the economic order includes the investigation of whether fair competition is violated. This is the case when there is price-fixing between sellers, information asymmetries between sellers and buyers, and negative externalities. "Negative externalities" is a term from economics. The effect occurs when companies operate at the expense of nature, humans or customers. Actually, the companies have to bear all the costs and include them in the price. Examples include disposing of waste, waste air or waste water in nature without using treatment or filtering facilities, or producing goods that break according to plan. Actually, the companies have to pay for the disposal costs and include them in the price. Then the increase in turnover from the new purchase of the broken goods would be offset by higher disposal costs.

The Antitrust Agency can establish further laws to protect fair competition in antitrust law and works with the economic auditors to do so. The economic auditors in turn report suspicious transactions to the Antitrust Agency.

182§210 Principles of economic order: BV Art. 94, KV Art.50

20.7.3.1 State audit[183]

Ministries and their state enterprises must keep their accounts through their profile in the Labour Directory and, if possible, digitise all economic transactions to avoid double entry and to allow auditors to access them remotely. Ministries and their authorities, offices or establishments are audited according to the requirements of the Social Market Economy, the Ministry of Labour and Stateorgnisation[184] . As soon as auditors find deficiencies, business consultants are called in to correct the deficiencies. If state property is to be sold or state enterprises privatised, the economic auditors must carry out an extraordinary audit and present the results at the following committee.

Checks are made to ensure that mineral resources are only exploited by state enterprises and that profits are properly transferred to the treasury of the Ministry of Finance.

20.7.3.2 Private sector audit[185]

Private companies can keep their accounts free of charge via the Labour Directory, but must have entered all the data required by law at least for the annual accounts. Companies of different sizes are audited differently. The laws of the Ministry of Labour are comparable to the following laws[186] , but adapted to the particular economic form in which a company operates. The scope of services consists of audits of financial statements, business valuations, reorganisation

183§158,3 Finances of the ministries: BV Art.183, §210.7 Principles of economic order
184Ministry of State Organisation - 4.3.1 Guardians of the Constitution
185§27.4 Common good, §217.4 Banks and insurance companies: BV Art. 98
186German Code of Public Accountants (Wirtschaftsprüferordnung): https://www.gesetze-im-internet.de/wipro/ German Commercial Code (Handelsgesetzbuch): https://www.gesetze-im-internet. de/hgb/ German Financial Investment Brokerage Ordinance (Finanzanlagenvermittlungsverordnung): https://www.gesetze-im-internet.de/finvermv/ German Brokerage and Property Development Ordinance (Makler- und Bauträgerverordnung): https://www.gesetze-im-internet.de/gewo_34cdv/MaBV.pdf German Budget Principles Act (Haushaltsgrundsätzegesetz): https://www.gesetze-im-internet.de/hgrg/

and insolvency plans, over-indebtedness, insolvency, embezzlement, international accounting, and the purchase, sale, incorporation, transformation or merger of companies or parts of companies. The department of business consultants can take over the preparation of the documents to be audited, but charges fees or taxes for this.

If a company becomes insolvent, the economic auditors have to check whether insolvency has occurred.[187]

20.7.3.3 Unfair working conditions

Government and private sector workers can indicate in the Company Auditing Agency's audit interviews if they feel they have been treated unfairly at work. If the report is justified, the economic auditor convenes a company committee and goes along to the meeting as an advocate for the affected employee. If the auditor detects an unfair business practice, he or she must report it to the responsible Minister of Economic Affairs. The minister can caution, punish or close the company.

20.7.3.4 Auditing in the Free Market Economy

In the Free Market Economy, only the tests that apply to all economic forms and are listed above for the private sector are applied. When trading their own shares or bonds on the stock exchange, the companies in the Free Market Economy must be audited to be ready for the stock exchange and pay an annual fee to the Exchange Commission. The payment of the appropriate fee is audited. The economic auditors are supported by the Antitrust Agency with auditors specialised in assessing free competition and breaking up oligopolies, monopolies and cartels. Where joint-stock companies are audited, staff from the Exchange Commission assist in the audit.

---

187 Ministry of Justice - 8.1.4 Insolvency delay

20.7.3.5 Auditing in the Social Market Economy

The economic auditors receive their requirements from the laws and instructions from the Ministry of Social Market Economy. In detail, the following areas are audited.

20.7.3.5.1 Non-profit audit

A Non-profit company is not allowed to pay out profits, but must reinvest them in the company, pay them out to all employees and give them back to the customers through discounts. If the supply situation is deficient and individual Non-profit companies become insolvent, the business auditors establish this fact and instruct the economic consultants to form a cartel.[188]

20.7.3.5.2 Audit of employment contract deadlines

If an employment relationship is to be limited in time, there must be a factual reason for it, which the economic auditors examine and rate. The rating determines whether the fixed-term contract is permissible.

20.7.3.5.3 Audit of the automation

By testing automation, the ratio of machines to workers is calculated on the final product. According to the results, the income flows into the Unconditional Basic Income as wages to the employees or as machine tax.

20.7.3.5.4 Real estate audit

Expert economic auditors of the building trade check the condition of the property before each sale and before each letting and publish the inspection report on the profile of the property in the Real Estate Directory.

---

188 Ministry of Social Market Economy - 11.2 Non-profit companies, 11.2.1 Cartels

20.7.3.5.5 Manager in internship

The economic auditors check managers to see whether and how they have completed their mandatory internships in the different areas of their company.

20.7.3.5.6 Audit of company sports opportunities

It is checked whether the company sport is stipulated in the duty roster to a sufficient extent during working hours and whether the exercise has been observed in accordance with the health requirements for the occupational group.

20.7.3.5.7 Audit of insolvency insurance fraud

In the case of an insurance benefit from the insolvency insurance, it is checked whether the owner has previously owned a company that became wholly or partially insolvent. The results are reported to the insolvency insurance company.

20.7.3.5.8 Audit before insurance benefits

If a building is damaged by a natural event, the amount of damage is examined in order to determine the compensation to be paid by the building insurance.

20.7.3.5.9 Avoiding waste

As soon as the company audits detect overproduction or disposal of returns, the economic auditors intervene in a regularisation capacity. All affected companies are gathered under the direction and moderation of the economic auditors to reach agreements on prices, quantities and market areas. The economic auditors take care to ensure equitable sharing and to avoid overproduction, shortages and waste. The negotiations are broadcast on Government Television[189] . Affected citizens can use a veto quorum of 10% to force companies and the

---

189Ministry of Media - 7 Government Television

Company Auditing Agency to reach agreements on quantities and prices publicly on Government Television or Local Television[190] with the participation of the Minister for Social Market Economy or his deputy minister.

20.7.3.5.10 Additional audit for business promotion

In the course of founding a company, after a reform to maximise profits or after an introduced innovation of research and development, companies can receive an additional audit. The business consultants take on the advice for start-up and profit maximisation, and the innovation auditors take on the advice for research and development.

20.7.3.5.11 Marketing success models

As soon as auditors recognise a success model or it is indicated to them by the company, they examine it closely and document it. The investigations are intended to measure and confirm the economic success of the measures. The entrepreneurs can instruct the auditors to profile the success model and include it in the Success Model Directory so that other companies can view and use the success model after paying a fee. The auditors propose the amount of the one-off fee and the entrepreneurs determine the final amount.[191]

If companies are interested in a success model but do not know whether it is suitable for them, they can ask the economic auditors. If the economic auditors find that a company is suitable for importing an existing success model, they make the entrepreneurs a free and non-binding offer.

190 Ministry of Media - 9 Local Television
191 Ministry of Social Market Economy - 17.2.1 Success model programme

20.7.3.5.11.1 Certification of success models

The company that has registered a success model is continuously checked to see if the success model continues to be successful. All companies that have purchased a success model are certified by the auditors as to whether they have properly implemented and are operating it. All participating companies take part in an ongoing study that measures how successful a success model is. If a success model is not successful in all participating companies, the deviations and their causes are reviewed. The success model must be deleted from the directory if success cannot be guaranteed or can no longer be guaranteed. Failure is determined jointly and unanimously by the auditors of the Company Auditing Agency. This means that only one Audit Department has to disprove the guarantee of success and deletion from the directory occurs. This also includes when a success model can benefit a company or its customers but damage humans or nature.

20.7.3.6 Auditing in the Planned Economy

The economic auditors audit the two work areas separately in the Planned Economy and pay attention to the different requirements for Planned Enterprise, Innovation Enterprise, Experimental Enterprise and People's Innovation Company.

20.7.3.6.1 First work area: basic supply

20.7.3.6.1.1 Audit of the need for workers in basic supply[192]

It is checked whether a job is necessary to fulfil the task or not. In the Planned Economy basic supply work area, all Social Village residents must work. The economic auditors make sure that everyone only has to work for as short a time as possible to ensure basic supply for all Social Villagers.

192Ministry of Planned Economy - 9.3.1 Recruitment in the basic supply

20.7.3.6.1.2 Audit of the duty roster[193]

All basic supply services are checked for their necessity. It is checked whether basic supply is guaranteed. This includes operations that provide residents with healthy food, clean clothing, water, sanitation, heat and shelter to live, work and gather at all times. It is determined in which cycles jobs can be shared to compensate for the fluctuating number of workers and consumers with an increase or decrease in the number of hours per week.

20.7.3.6.1.3 Operational and business research

Suggestions for improvement are examined during staff interviews. If a proposal could increase the efficiency of the basic supply, a pilot test must be undertaken. If efficiency has been increased, all affected companies must undertake a pilot and, if successful, retain the improvement proposal and add it to the success model database. The economic auditors investigate the success of the pilot tests and enter successful improvement proposals in the database of success models.

20.7.3.6.1.4 Audit of working hours[194]

The economic auditors receive a description from the employers of the work to be done per hour, together with ratings from the employees. From this, the economic auditors calculate a requirement so that a digital duty roster can be created and virtually simulated. In the audit result, the work performance per hour is stated. This audit takes place for the companies of both work areas.

---

193 Ministry of Planned Economy - 7.6 Duty roster
194 Ministry of Planned Economy - 13.2 Digital currency Working

20.7.3.6.2 Second work area: luxury supply

20.7.3.6.2.1 Audit of the need for workers in luxury supply[195]

It is checked whether a job is necessary to fulfil the task or not. In the luxury supply work area of the Planned Economy, all residents of the Social Villages can work. Therefore, in the luxury supply work area, many will work based on their interests and also have time for in-service training to obtain necessary qualifications. Overemployment may occur because the payment of wages is not necessary. The economic auditors check young companies for market readiness and tell entrepreneurs how far they are from market readiness and what steps would be necessary.

The economic auditors ensure that each job is checked to see if it is necessary to provide a good or service, or if other work processes can accomplish the service with the same or fewer workers or machines. The auditor's calculation is automatically linked to costs of items by the extension programme and the measure is simulated by the Algoracle. The items can be goods or workers that are available as goods in the Procurement Office or as workers in the Labour Directory with the appropriate qualification in the occupational field that have a certain wage in the profile. The check result shows the companies how much the measure might cost and how long it will take. The business consultants are responsible for implementing the measures together with the companies.

20.7.3.6.2.2 Measurement of currency Working hours[196]

The economic auditors ensure the measurement of currency working hours in the Planned Economy using the human capital factor. When Social Villagers provide goods or services for each other in the two work areas, the demander owes time to the supplier. If both have had to undergo similar amounts of

---

195 Ministry of Planned Economy - 10.3.1 Recruitment in the luxury supply
196 Ministry of Planned Economy - 13.2 Digital currency Working hours

training, have similar levels of responsibility at work, or have to master similar levels of difficulty to perform the service, they owe each other the same amount of time.

The training hours are counted as a percentage of the working hours via a multiplier. Those who have had longer training thus receive a larger share of the working hours additionally credited. The Ministry of Education states how long an educational qualification takes on average. From this, the Company Auditing Agency calculates the education factor, which is multiplied by the working hours to reflect the time share for the duration of the training. In addition to education, human capital also includes the factors for responsibility and difficulty that arise in a job. The responsibility factors are proposed by the economic auditors, the difficulty factors by the health auditors. The proposals for the factors are voted on by the employees in the wage negotiations. The education, responsibility and difficulty factors together make up the human capital factor.

The factors of the humans working for each other are offset against each other so that it is clear who owes whom how many working hours. The services of the Planned Economy can thus also be paid for with counter-performances. The economic auditors check the working time accounts on the profiles of the persons in the Social Directory.

20.7.3.6.2.3 Audit of Innovation Enterprises[197]

If a new Innovation Enterprise is to be established, it is examined whether there is a shortage of the new good or service in the market economy and whether the prices are higher than those of the Innovation Enterprise. Firstly, the test involves digitally querying all the business figures of all the competitor companies in the market economy in order to calculate the market entry costs. The competitors' business figures are used to simulate the outcome of a price war between established and new market participants. In this way, the auditors virtually estimate the risk of default on payment. Second, competitors' local and national sales figures are used to capture the level

197 Ministry of Planned Economy - 10.6 Innovation Enterprise

and variability of demand. Using data from the Ministry of Foreign Affairs, global demand is estimated and can be output for each country individually.

Auditors check which skilled workers are needed and which Social Villagers have the qualifications or who might be interested in attending in-service training at the Social Village's educational institutions while working in the Innovation Enterprise. The auditors can recommend existing employees to attend in-service training.

The innovation auditors stop payments from the Innovation Fund if the payments are not sufficient to bring the company to market maturity or no cost-covering operation in the other two economic forms can be possible. This judgement can only be decided jointly by all auditors after an overall audit. The Innovation Enterprise must announce insolvency and close down. Procurements must be resold if possible. The proceeds flow back to the Innovation Fund.

20.7.3.6.2.4 Sharing success models[198]

If success models are identified during the audit, they are discussed with the innovation auditors and included in the Success Model Directory or a suitable industrial property right is registered. All companies and enterprises of the Planned Economy share all their success models with each other free of charge. Success models from other economic forms must be paid for. Companies of other economic forms have to pay for success models of Planned Economy enterprises. The economic auditors take care of the distribution in the suitable companies and establishments of the Planned Economy as well as the marketing in the Social Market Economy and Free Market Economy.

---

198 Ministry of Planned Economy - 10.4.3 Licences for success models

20.7.3.6.2.5 Audit of profit sharing[199]

If an employee has indicated in the questionnaire that he or she believes he or she is unfairly or not at all involved in profits, the employee's pay and bonuses will be reviewed and compared with other similar employees. If lower pay cannot be justified by lower performance, the amounts must be compensated retroactively.

20.7.3.6.2.6 Audit of unfair working conditions

If unfair labour practices are reported, the economic auditors will convene a company committee and represent the affected employee, who can remain anonymous if they wish. If an unfair business practice is found, the auditor can order the company to refrain from such actions in the future and report the incident to the Minister for Planned Economy.

20.7.3.6.2.7 Payments from the Innovation Fund

It is audited how much money was taken from which Innovation Enterprise and for what purpose. Disbursements from the fund are only transferred to an Innovation Enterprise by the economic auditors after a successful overall audit. In the regular audits, the proper use of the money is checked and new disbursements can be initiated. If the money could not achieve the desired purpose, further payments are stopped and the operating licence is withdrawn.

20.7.3.7 Auditing in the Barter Economy

20.7.3.7.1 Determining the demand

Through the information provided by the residents of a Barter Economy Zone, a plenary assembly[200] determines how demand has been met since the previous audit. The demand

---

199 Ministry of Planned Economy - 10.4.1 Profit Sharing
200 Ministry of Barter Economy - 7.2 Plenary Assembly

for basic needs and leisure activities is recorded separately. On the basis of visits, working practices are recorded and documented. The audit results tell residents how well they are meeting their demand, which goods, devices and services find frequent demand as a strong currency in the Barter Economy Zone, and with which division of labour the Barter Economy Zone can develop the most benefits for all residents of the Barter Economy Zone.

20.7.3.7.2 Audit of the environmental impact

The economic auditors carry out unannounced and covert inspections[201] together with the health and legality auditors. They are trained for this by the health auditors and can have samples checked by the Institute for Environmental Protection. These inspections relate to the requirement to use only naturally rapidly degradable substances in the Barter Economy Zone and to import them from the surrounding area into the Barter Economy Zone. They also refer to the requirement to use only as many raw materials as will grow back in the Barter Economy Zone.

Anyone who is proven to have violated a commandment must move out of the Barter Economy. If culprits cannot be identified, a committee is convened to determine who must leave the Barter Economy Zone and what precautions should be taken to prevent similar things from happening in the future. The economic auditors investigate whether there are other ways in other Barter Economy Zones that lead to a similar result in the long term. These methods are tested and, if they prove successful, included in the Success Model Directory.

---

201 Ministry of Barter Economy - 9.4.1 Inspection

20.7.3.7.3 Audit of imports and exports

Most often, economic auditors for the Barter Economy work in an office of the wholesale market[202] in the capital city of a Barter Economy Zone. There they audit goods and services that non-Better Economy suppliers want to offer. Any materials must be compostable that are imported into the Barter Economy Zone. Traders who want to repeatedly offer their goods in the wholesale market can have their goods certified and thus assure that the service always meets the requirements. Random samples are taken and examined.

The economic auditors determine the zone in the wholesale market where only compliant items can be found and where residents of the Barter Economy Zone are allowed to shop. For vendors in the wholesale market who are residents of the Barter Economy Zone, checks are made to ensure that their export of goods does not overburden the renewable resources or take them away from the residents.

20.7.4 Technical auditor

The technical auditors report to the Ministry of Innovation and test products, machine guidance and industrial plants neutrally, objectively and with an open mind. They comply with the laws of the Ministry of Labour, which are comparable to the regulation on safety and health protection in the use of work equipment.[203] They inspect work equipment, such as equipment, tools and machines, as well as goods and services for their condition and execution. Driving licence tests are taken for the operation of certain machines. The technical auditors determine which machines these are as part of their product testing. If the operation of a product proves to be potentially dangerous to humans and nature as long as it is not used properly, then a driving licence obligation is to be proposed by the technical auditors to the Minister of Labour. The Ministry of Labour may enact the duty as a law. Similarly, technical auditors may set inspection intervals for products

202 Ministry of Barter Economy - 10.2.2 Wholesale Market
203 https://www.gesetze-im-internet.de/betrsichv_2015/index.
html#BJNR004910015BJNE000402126

and equipment to be tested to determine whether they are still safe and fit for use after prolonged use or non-use.

The technical auditors are not only deployed at the regular testing appointments, but also in the event of accidents, damage investigations and for the accompanying development of new products and major projects.

The technical auditors can open up further testing areas as soon as they discover them. They report their proposals to the Institute for Evaluation, which develops new audit criteria and procedures in cooperation with the Institute of Technology.[204]

20.7.4.1 Qualification of the auditors

The technical auditors are engineers, chemists, physicists, computer scientists, ecotrophologists, psychologists or biologists. These scientists are employees of the Ministry of Education when they are not working for the Company Auditing Agency. Other staff of the technical auditors are employees of the Patent Office, the Innovation Agency and employees of the Ministry of Digital Affairs for hardware and software security. The Ministry of Education, together with the Institute of Technology, offers further training measures to become an expert.

20.7.4.2 Seal of approval

The PS (Proven Safety) test seal is issued at the first test, which may include a date for a test interval and expiry. Buyers must be able to identify the inspection subject and grade on the inspection seal, if necessary online by scanning the barcode. If goods, services or work equipment are subject to continuous testing, manufacturers must indicate this at the time of sale and provide information on frequency, duration and price. The inspection seal is withdrawn if the requirements can no longer be met.

The CE (Conformitée Européenne / European Conformity) test seal is used for the import of goods. Both seals are only

---

204 Ministry of Innovation - 7.1 Institute of Technology

awarded by the auditors if safety, sustainability and quality can be guaranteed by the auditors' tests for health and technology. The import of drugs is only permitted if the health auditors have checked compliance with the purity requirement[205] and confirm purity. Only when this confirmation has been received is the testing for the CE seal carried out.

20.7.4.2.1 Labelling for consumer protection

It is checked whether the labelling obligations for consumer protection are complied with and the information is correct. The technical auditors, if necessary with or through other auditors of the Company Auditing Agency, control the compliance with the price indication, indication of origin, environmental traffic light, food traffic light and the Social Market Economy quality label.

20.7.4.3 Acceptance of test procedures from manufacturers

First and foremost, manufacturers are obliged to ensure safety and suitability for use. Therefore, manufacturers must submit their own tests of their new goods, services and work equipment to the technical auditors. These tests should include information on which instructions for use are necessary and on the service life for which the performance is designed. The service life must be guaranteed for as long as the environmental impact of the production and use of a product is no longer negative. For example, the production of a smartphone involves such a strong impact on the environment that it would have to be used for 200 years. Similar calculations exist for paper bags and plastic bags. The smartphone example shows that individual components must be upgradable and repairable and should be made of renewable raw materials if possible. The technical auditors can prescribe further test procedures to the manufacturers. These procedures and their results are checked by the Institute of Technology in cooperation with the technical auditors.

---

205 Ministry of Health - 5.11.2 Purity Law

20.7.4.4 Cooperation with state enterprises

The technical auditors provide advice to the state enterprises and prepare plans for construction projects or products. The state enterprises can have the tests and the development of the test procedures carried out by the department of technical auditors.[206]

20.7.4.5 Equipment inspection

Employers must notify the technical auditors when new work equipment requiring testing is used, in order to check that it is installed properly and, if necessary, to test the affected employees in handling it. If work processes of a service are to be or have to be certified, the employers report this and receive a regular inspection by the technical auditors. Measuring instruments in use at work are regularly checked by comparative measurements and receive a seal with the year in which they must be recalibrated.

20.7.4.6 Product testing

During product testing, type, random samples, production sites, safety for humans and nature, usability and service quality are examined, tested and documented. With the test result, the grades as well as the average grade of all individual tests are listed. Only the average score is shown on the test seal. The full test report of each product is given on its profile page in the Labour Directory. If the product is new and a patent application has been filed, the Patent Office staff member who conducted the patent examination also conducts the product examination.

---

206 Ministry of Innovation - 10.3 Construction projects, 10.3.1 Planning

20.7.4.7 Private examinations

Once every 12 months, the technical auditors offer to test devices belonging to private individuals. These test dates are indicated in the local waste calendar and take place in suitable workshops either provided by companies or state institutions such as educational institutions or intranet cafés. At these audit appointments, citizens' own items are audited. These inspections are free of charge for residents of the Social Village.

20.7.5 Innovation auditor[207]

The innovation auditors report to the Ministry of Innovation and consist of staff from the Patent Office and the Innovation Agency.[208] They abide by the laws of the Ministry of Innovation and are committed to raising human living standards through technical and moral progress. They audit companies for innovations and assist in their development.

The innovation auditors are at the same time notaries and advisors for innovations. They are subject to special confidentiality, the breach of which is punishable by imprisonment. Their services are subject to a fee for companies in the Social Market Economy and Free Market Economy, although the first 3 years after founding the company are always free of charge. Foreigner companies are not allowed to receive advice from the innovation auditors.

20.7.5.1 Innovation audit

Innovation auditors know where there is potential for improvement because they audit and advise so many companies in an industry. If they detect deficiencies, they tell the companies. The innovation auditors also check new work processes, goods or services that originate from ideas and suggestions for improvement from employees or from the innovation meeting[209] with persons from outside the company.

---

207 §183,1,2 Research and innovation: BV Art. 64
208 Ministry of Innovation - 7.3 Patent Office, 4 Innovation Agency
209 Ministry of Innovation - 9.8 Innovation meeting

On the one hand, the companies themselves collect this data and make it available to the auditors. On the other hand, the Company Auditing Agency issues questionnaires to all employees at every audit. The parts with questions about ideas and suggestions for improvement are sent to the innovation auditors and checked for feasibility. Feasible innovations are then entered into the company's Innovation Database.

20.7.5.2 Notary's office

The innovation auditors ensure that innovations in companies are recognised and notarised. They identify innovative processes and propose to companies to include these processes in the Innovation Database.

When a company is audited by the innovation auditors, innovative trade secrets and the company's own patents or other industrial property rights are also notarised and certified in the audit report. Employees of the companies can also preliminarily record innovations themselves with their People's Computer in the meantime of two examinations. To do this, they save them in their Innovation Database at least 2 weeks before the examination. In the examination, this data is then notarised. The auditors always ask whether they may also offer the data to other companies for a fee.

20.7.5.3 Innovation programme

The innovation programme is an extension of the audit programme and the advisory programme. Innovation auditors use it every time they audit companies. The Innovation Programme is used to enable algorithms to combine data from the Innovation Database, Success Model Directory, Labour Directory and Ideas Directory[210] in the service of the Company Auditing Agency.

The market opportunities of all innovations are automatically checked individually for each company that uses or wants to use them. For this purpose, the introduction of the innovation

---

210 Ministry of Innovation - 8 Ideas Directory

is simulated by the Algoracle .[211]

Innovation auditors check whether an innovation can be protected by the Ministry of Innovation. When an innovation is added to the Innovation Database, it is automatically checked whether industrial property rights already exist for it and which industrial property right would be suitable for the innovation. The programme carries out this investigation automatically by algorithms searching the directories for ideas, success models and labour for comparable entries or suitable industrial property rights. If a protection option is available, the innovation auditors suggest that the entrepreneur apply for the possible industrial property right at the Patent Office. The results of this automatic investigation are stated in the examination report.

During each audit, companies are examined to see if there is room for improvement. Because the innovation auditors visit so many companies, they know many paths that have led to success or failure. If they identify shortcomings, they enter them into the innovation programme and automatically receive proposals as to which existing innovations or success models and which existing or expired industrial property rights might be suitable to remedy the shortcomings. In the audit report, all deficiencies are indicated and all possibilities that exist to eliminate the deficiencies.

20.7.5.4 Innovation promotion

The Company Auditing Agency promotes innovation through the innovation auditors and their audit of new innovative goods, services and business processes. This audit can be ordered by entrepreneurs up to 2 weeks before the audit date or at any time. If innovation auditors discover innovations during their routine audit, they enter them in the Innovation Database.

In order to increase the productivity of as many companies as possible, the innovation auditors offer suitable innovations from the Ideas Directory, the Innovation Database and success models from the Success Model Directory in the

211 Ministry of Digital Affairs - 15.3 Algoracle

audit report. Depending on the economic form, the offer is free of charge or subject to a fee. Companies in the Planned Economy share everything free of charge, companies in the Social Market Economy share everything they want free of charge, companies in the Barter Economy and Free Market Economy share everything they want for a fee.

If employees of a company have expressed the innovations via the questionnaire, the Company Auditing Agency informs them of this in the audit report and does not charge any costs for this. On the contrary, the company or the employee receives a proposal to market the innovation.

20.7.5.4.1 Approval of funds from the Innovation Fund[212]

Companies that want to implement innovations but do not have enough money to do so can receive money from the Innovation Fund.[213] To do so, they submit a motions to the innovation auditors. The motions should state what costs will be incurred and why this is necessary in order to implement the innovation. The innovation auditors examine the application together with the economic auditors. The auditors discuss the results with the entrepreneurs and can make improvements and savings and amend the motions. If the application is in mutual agreement, the money from the Innovation Fund is paid out as soon as a receipt is received. Bridging loans between purchase and receipt disbursement are provided by the People's Bank for companies in the Barter Economy, Planned Economy and Social Market Economy. The subsequent Company Auditing Agency audit of this company will verify that all receipts are for the agreed purpose of implementation of the innovation. Funds that have been used improperly must be repaid within 12 months. If improper use occurs again, increasingly more monetary fines become due or payments from the Innovation Fund become impossible.

The innovation auditors use the audit to find out how much additional profit has been generated by an innovation. From the fifth year onwards, 5% of this share flows into the

212§183.5 Research and innovation
213Ministry of Innovation - 9.11.1.1 Innovation Fund

Innovation Fund each year. If licensors have issued licence participation shares[214] , the licence fee is deducted from the licensee's profit share and transferred to the shareholders as a dividend.

20.7.5.4.2 Measuring the profit share through innovations

The share of profits generated by the innovations since the last audit is examined. The data for the calculations come from the responsible economic auditors. The share of profits is shown as a percentage and the absolute amount is shown in a valid national currency in the audit report.

If the innovations are proprietary to the company, the proposal is to issue licence participation shares. Even if companies do not grant licences to other companies at all, they can be the sole licensee and the owners of the shares become the licensor. In this way, innovations can be brought to the Ideas Stock Exchange[215] . The readiness for the Ideas Stock Exchange is checked by the innovation auditors in voting with the Exchange Commission.

20.7.5.5 Promotion of research and development

The expenditure and efforts of the companies on research and development are audited. By entering the innovation programme, other audited companies in the country that are pursuing similar research and development are automatically listed. In the auditor's report, the auditors propose to the companies to combine their projects in order to achieve synergy effects. If companies agree, the names are given to the entrepreneurs and contact is made. The companies that did not agree do not receive any notifications. The auditing software also examines all state research projects at the universities and (high) schools and proposes cooperation to the Ministry of Education.[216] If all participants agree, contact is established. Companies that do not agree do not participate

214 Ministry of Finance - 11.9.3 Licence shares
215 Ministry of Finance - 11.9 Ideas Stock Exchange
216 Ministry of Education - 11.7.1 Research community

in the cooperation.

20.7.5.5.1 Approval of funds from the Research Cost Fund[217]

If there is not enough money for research and development projects, money from the Research Cost Fund can be applied for from the innovation auditors. This application must list the costs and the resulting benefits. The economic auditors check the costs and the innovation auditors check the benefits. Both give an assessment of whether the benefit justifies these costs or whether the same or similar thing can also be achieved more cheaply.

If the pots are closed, the audit results are communicated to the companies involved, which decide on the disbursements. If the pots are open, the innovation auditors decide on the payments.

20.7.5.6 Approval of the relaxations of antitrust law

Innovation Enterprises of the Planned Economy and companies of the Social Market Economy are examined as to whether they are entitled to a relaxation of antitrust law. Provided that innovations have been audited or joint innovations and projects for research and development are exported, the antitrust law can be temporarily relaxed. The relaxation is only permissible if the introduction of an innovation is so expensive that a company could become insolvent or overindebted in free competition. Economic auditors take over this examination as soon as the innovation auditors give them the order and transmit the necessary data. First, the relaxation provides that domestic companies in the Planned Economy, Social Market Economy and Free Market Economy Innovation Communities can establish[218] to agree on price fixing, purchasing cooperation, non-compete obligations, exclusive purchasing or supply obligations or market sharing with each other. Antitrust Agency staff must

---

217 Ministry of Innovation - 5.3.1 Research Cost Fund
218 Ministry of Innovation - 9.10.1 Innovation Community (IC)

attend all such meetings and have a veto right. This veto power allows them to renegotiate or prohibit agreements. In the Free Market Economy, the relaxation of antitrust law is only allowed if companies cooperate with a People's Innovation Company.

Secondly, the relaxation provides that domestic Planned Economy and Social Market Economy companies can jointly sell an innovation on the world market if they could not economically afford it on their own. The innovation auditors examine the innovation and the economic auditors examine the economic productivity of all individual companies. If both come to the conclusion that an export oligopoly[219] achieves the necessary profits to refinance the innovation at 120%, this is noted in the audit report. Companies can use the report to obtain a temporary relaxation from the Antitrust Agency.

20.7.5.7 Request to become a People's Innovation Company

During the first audit of new companies, the innovation auditors[220] examine whether the company markets an innovation that benefits the population, is in high demand worldwide and could generate monopoly profits due to high willingness to pay. If the company meets the requirements, the innovation auditors note this in the audit report and send their findings to the Innovation Agency. The Innovation Agency makes an offer to the affected entrepreneurs to become a People's Innovation Company. Otherwise, People's Innovation Companies receive the same treatment from the innovation auditors as Social Market Economy companies.

20.7.6 Legality auditor

The legality auditors report to the ministries of labour, security and justice. The Ministry of Labour sends staff from the Antitrust Agency, the Ministry of Security sends staff from the Police, Customs and the Ministry of Justice sends prosecutors

---

219 Ministry of Innovation - 9.10.2 Export Oligopoly
220 Ministry of Innovation - 10.1 Initiators

for criminal and economic law. The legality auditors ensure that the auditors of the Company Auditing Agency work conscientiously and incorruptibly, and that the criminal laws for persons and companies, antitrust law and the prevention of economic crime are observed.

The auditors enforce the company's criminal law[221] and are authorised to collect immediate monetary fines, file charges, make arrests and seizures if relevant deficiencies are found by them or other auditors. They become active if auditors suspect a criminal offence during an audit and report the incident. The auditors may have suspicions themselves or may assume suspicions to be checked through the statements of employees and entrepreneurs in the questionnaires.

The auditors ensure compliance with and enforcement of the rules, constitution, laws and standards. In this way, they take on the task of internal revision for state and corporate activities in the country.

20.7.6.1 Company Auditing Agency work audit

Police officers examine the work of the other auditors of the Company Auditing Agency. In doing so, they make sure that confidentiality is respected and whether there are any attempts at bribery.[222] Employees of the companies can turn to them if they suspect unlawful conduct by the auditors. Anyone who notices bribery or a breach of confidentiality by Company Auditing Agency auditors can file a report with the police, who will investigate the case.

20.7.6.2 Audit of constitutional law[223]

Public prosecutors for constitutional law examine whether companies and their business practices violate fundamental rights, i.e. damage the common good. They are supported in

---

221 Ministry of Justice - 8.1.3 Corporate criminal law
222 Ministry of Justice - 8.1.1 Company Auditing Agency confidentiality, 8.1.2 Bribery
223 §27,3,5 Common good, §210 Principles of economic order : BV Art. 94, KV Art.50

their examination by the Guardians of the Constitution[224] by checking dubious business practices for their compliance with the Constitution. If compliance with the constitution is not guaranteed, charges are filed.

20.7.6.3 Audit of administrative procedural law

Employees of the Internal Service of the Federal Moderator's Office[225] check whether all ministries and their authorities comply with the requirements of the Administrative Procedure Act. For this purpose, the function of the internal heterarchy is audited, the administration and the state employees. In the case of state employees, the requirements and remuneration are examined.[226]

20.7.6.4 Compliance with commercial law

Customs officers check the import and export of goods by the company.[227] In the case of imports from foreigners, they ensure that tariffs have been paid and that only permissible goods have been imported. The ministries of economy determine the corresponding requirements in their foreign trade regulations. Legality auditors check whether the goods have received the necessary Company Auditing Agency seals of approval and whether they are counterfeit and pirated. If piracy is found, the legality auditors open a preliminary investigation against the buyer and seller. They hand the case over to the police and, if it is foreigner piracy, to Customs. They monitor the import ban on counterfeits, lethal weapons and goods harmful to human health. The Ministry of Health determines which goods are harmful to human health and nature and advises the customs officers in case of doubt.[228]

When exporting goods to foreign countries, it is checked

---

224 Ministry of State Organisation - 4.3.1 Guardians of the Constitution
225 Ministry of State Organisation - 4.4 Federal Moderator's Office
226 Ministry of State Organisation - 8.4.3 Internal heterarchy, 9.8.5 Administration, 8.4.4 State employees
227 Ministry of Security - 8 Customs
228 Ministry of Security - 8.2.10 Import of goods

whether the goods do not originate from the Barter Economy or Planned Economy. If goods from companies in the Social Market Economy have been given a poor quality certificate by the technical auditors, they may not be exported. The export of weapons is prohibited as long as they are not sold to states with which there is a defence alliance and a peace treaty.[229]

20.7.6.5 Tax Investigation Department

Customs Tax Investigation Departments follow up on leads and conduct investigations.[230] Indications of tax evasion, dummy companies, loss-making subsidiaries or undeclared work[231] , reported by auditors of the Company Auditing Agency or users in the Labour Directory, are investigated. If the suspicion is confirmed, more Tax Investigation Department officers are requested as reinforcement and the company is directly searched or secretly monitored.

20.7.6.6 Sabotage protection

Employees of the Constitutional Court and prosecutors of the appropriate Remit Courts are legality auditors for sabotage protection. For sabotage protection, suspicious persons who prepare criminal offences in the course of their activities are investigated. In this way, legality auditors provide security monitoring of companies, state enterprises and ministries. Together with the Minister of Security, they formulate the Security Clearance Act[232] and submit it to the people for voting.

20.7.6.7 Data protection

Legality auditors examine data protection arrangements. In the course of the audit, all measures and devices used to process and store person-related data are examined. The

229 Ministry of Security - 8.2.12 Export of goods
230 Ministry of Security - 8.3 Tax Investigation Department
231 Ministry of Security - 8.3.2.2 Undeclared work
232 https://www.gesetze-im-internet.de/s_g/

legality auditors for the audit of devices for digital data processing are employees from the Institute for Information Security[233] . They check on the one hand whether the data are effectively protected and on the other hand whether they are being misused. In the case of unannounced audits, brief cyberattacks are carried out on the company in advance.[234]

20.7.6.8 Compliance with labour law

Legality auditors of the Ministry of Labour check the generally binding rules in labour law. Questionnaires and visual inspections are used to examine whether psychological pressure is exerted on employees or whether employees are treated unequally or unfairly, lie to customers, colleagues or superiors, act with gross negligence or have to deceive fraudulently. Superiors who are found to have made false promises are investigated to see if they are only paid the wage level of the affected subordinate.

Employment contracts of new employees since the last audit are reviewed. It is examined whether the collectively agreed wage or the minimum wage, the working hours and job description have been complied with.

For goods and services, it is checked that the General Terms and Conditions (GTC) are no longer than 2 A4 pages with a maximum of 1500 characters per page.

In order to verify the right to have fun at work, the questionnaires are evaluated and, if necessary, changes are enforced. The legality auditors head the committees and can issue binding rules for the companies in voting with the workforce.[235]

The state enterprises and private companies are audited to determine whether there is nepotism, favouritism or blasphemy and bullying. The audit is conducted through the questionnaires and oral examinations of the plaintiffs and interrogations of the defendants by police officers. The legality

233 Ministry of Digital Affairs - 8.1 Institute for Information Security
234 Ministry of Digital Affairs - 8.2 Cyber Defence
235 Ministry of Justice - 8.1.3 Corporate criminal law, 8.1.3.4 False promises, 8.1.6 Right to have fun at work, 8.1.5 General Terms and Conditions (GTC)

auditors determine the severity of the guilt and thus guideline values for the sentence through the audit results of all auditors and audits of the company.[236]

The visas of foreign workers are checked and in case of visa overstay, the affected worker is arrested and deported. The company receives a monetary fine. Customs officers carry out the check.[237]

20.7.6.9 Compliance with antitrust law

Antitrust Agency employees are legality auditors for antitrust law. Undercover examinations are carried out to uncover unfair competition, price agreements, information asymmetries or negative externalities. If suspicions are confirmed, Antitrust Agency staff are called in as reinforcements and investigate the company. If fines or pre-trial detention are imposed, the legality auditors enforce this immediately.

20.7.6.10 Enforcement of innovation law

Prosecutors for patent and commercial law of the Ministry of Justice are legality auditors for innovation law. They check whether products break faster according to plan. In case of suspicion, the legality auditors initiate an examination by the technical auditors. They check whether innovations are being suppressed. This is the case if entrepreneurs are in possession of an industrial property right that would make the company's business model completely or partially obsolete. This industrial property right can be expropriated by the legality auditors and become common property.

Special checks are provided for in cases of suspected procrastination of innovation. Auditors check whether outdated production methods are used or invested in, although newer production methods are available that are more beneficial to the standard of living or the health of humans and nature. Suspected cases are investigated more

236Ministry of Justice - 8.16.3 Nepotism, 8.16.4 Favouritism, 8.16.5 Blasphemy
237Ministry of Justice - 8.18.1 Visa overstay for guest workers

closely by the health auditors and economic auditors.

In the first audit, the facts of the procrastination of innovation are listed as a deficiency in the audit report and a deadline is set for when the deficiency must be remedied. The duration of the deadline is set by the economic auditors and depends on the amount of the company's profits. If the deadline is not met, a monetary fine becomes due, payable monthly and amounting to 50% of the monthly profits. The monetary fines are saved and can be used to hire the Company Auditing Agency's business consultants. The fine procedure ends after a period set by the technical auditors. After this period, the insolvency delay is considered intentional and will be prosecuted under criminal law.[238]

20.7.6.11 Enforcement of insolvency law

Ministry of Security police officers are legality auditors for insolvency law. If a company has debts, the legality auditors can seize cash and valuables. To do so, they need a court order, which creditors can obtain by filing a complaint with the police. If economic auditors detect an insolvency delay, the legality auditors conduct initial investigations.[239]

20.7.6.12 Implementation of the expropriation[240]

When a company is compulsorily expropriated, the legality auditors form the transitional board and fill all necessary vacancies with expert business consultants from the Company Auditing Agency.[241] The transitional board and all Company Auditing Agency staff withdraw from involvement in a nationalised company as soon as a court orders it and the Ministry of Labour has converted the company into a state enterprise and assigned it to the appropriate ministry. The return to the owners takes place as soon as the disposal costs

---

238 Ministry of Justice - 8.1.3 Corporate criminal law, 8.1.4 Insolvency delay
239 Ministry of Justice - 8.1.4 Insolvency delay
240 §25,2 Property guarantee: BV Art.26
241 Ministry of Justice - 8.1.3 Corporate criminal law

are covered. If the company can no longer generate profits to cover the disposal costs, it is closed and sold. The proceeds go towards covering the disposal costs.

If an owner is expropriated because a majority of the people claim ownership in a voting, they must be fully compensated. The amount of compensation is determined by the auditors of the Company Auditing Agency and an assessor chosen by the owner. In principle, it is based on the value of the property and the value of the expenditure incurred by the owner in order to obtain a replacement and to cope with the loss. The same applies to restrictions on the rights to use the property.

20.7.7 Business consultant[242]

The business consultants report to the Ministry of Labour. They advise ministries and state enterprises if affected citizens request it in votes, but at least once every 10 years. They provide advice to companies when requested to do so by companies or auditors of the Company Auditing Agency. The advisory service may have different purposes, such as establishment, purchasing, innovation, profit maximisation and insolvency. The Ministry of Labour can offer performance-based advisory services in affected municipalities to promote structures.

The Company Auditing Agency is made up of the best auditors of the People's Innovation Company, who have already audited well performing large and small companies and in their other professional activities have themselves successfully managed companies such as state enterprises, PICs or companies from as many economic forms as possible. These experienced managers gather a team around them. It consists of auditors from the Company Auditing Agency who have already audited the affected company, students, teachers, scientists, successful retired entrepreneurs, and ministry staff. The Ministry of Labour pays for the advice. Payment for the consultancy services is due in the event of success, deducted proportionately from profits and can extend over up to 5 years.

---

242 §212.3 Structural policy

20.7.7.1 Management consultancy assignment

Any entrepreneur may place an order with the Company Auditing Agency for a company audit. The orders should be received at least one week before the Company Auditing Agency's routine audit. The audit will then be more extensive, longer and with more staff.

The business consultants appear at the company no later than 4 weeks after the audit. For 5 days they observe and listen, collect data, gain an impression of the working atmosphere among entrepreneurs and employees. After 7 days, a company committee follows. There, the results are discussed, proposals are determined and a catalogue of measures is agreed upon, which the company would like to achieve by an agreed audit date.

20.7.7.2 Corporate governance

The business consultants are able to manage a company themselves for a short time if necessary. This is the case if a minister for labour or the economy orders it or if the entrepreneurs ask for it. Companies may ask for this because they are no longer able to do so themselves, for example because they lack knowledge or experience or because the employees have implemented a vote of no confidence or a strike. Corporate governance by the advisors is basically democratic.

20.7.7.3 Company committee

In the company committee, the business consultants discuss their findings with the entrepreneurs and employees, jointly identify problems as problems and look for solutions and ways of solving them with equal voting rights for employees and entrepreneurs. Business consultants moderate the company committee and, if necessary, invite experts for a fee. The procedure of a company committee is similar to the committee[243] . The minister and ministry are replaced by the

---

243 Ministry of State Organisation - 9.6 Committee

owners and executive superiors. The citizens are replaced by the employees of the company.

A company committee does not have to be carried out by the business consultants, this can also be done by economic auditors or the companies themselves. What is crucial is that the committee procedure is used and only the roles are replaced by a different group of persons.

20.7.7.4 Advisory programme

The counselling programme is installed on a device equipped like a People's Computer. It is registered as a second device on the counsellor and may only be used for official purposes. It consists of a user interface and numerous algorithms and linkers to all pages and directories of the intranet. It is designed to generate statistics from all Company Auditing Agency audits for any company operating inland and to simulate the past, present and future behaviour of entire markets. Through the programme, the advisers are able to track individual measures taken by companies that have had, are having or will have good or bad effects individually or collectively.

20.7.7.5 Purchasing department

The Purchasing Department takes care of the procurement of the products and works together with the Procurement Office for this purpose. In the process, collective orders for several companies should enable more favourable prices for the products. Goods and services are often needed to remedy deficiencies from the deficiency list. For certain deficiencies, tried and tested goods and services are already deposited with the procurement department. If companies need to purchase additional goods and services for advice, these orders also go through the purchasing department. Advisors can give the purchasing department access to the record of where the companies have been purchasing and when. The purchasing department checks the quantities, prices, quality and delivery times. Suppliers that are better than the purchasing department can be added to their inventory. Suppliers that are worse are shown to the companies and a better offer is made by the purchasing department.

20.7.7.6 Consulting services

The companies can select individual advisory services from the list below or combine them.

20.7.7.6.1 Carrying out the rectification of defects

If a company wishes to have deficiencies rectified by the Company Auditing Agency after the Company Auditing Agency audit, the business consultants will carry out these measures. Individual or all deficiencies can be eliminated. For the assignment, the advisors temporarily take over the management of the enterprise or only the management in individual departments.

20.7.7.6.2 Support for setting up a business

If companies to be newly established wish to receive advice before and during their establishment, the business consultants are available to assist them for 12 months. In their work, the business consultants draw on the procedures for setting up companies in the Social Market Economy.[244] In voting with the entrepreneurs, measures are carried out, discussed and implemented.

The market analysis shows the market environment, i.e. which company offers a similar good or service where at what average price and what the average costs are. Advisors and entrepreneurs decide where the company should serve which clientele. The business analysis consists of the business plan, which is worked out with the entrepreneurs, and an initial company audit by all auditors of the Company Auditing Agency. If nothing is available apart from the business plan,

---

244 Ministry of Social Market Economy - 17.1 Setting up a business, Ministry of Planned Economy - 10.6 Innovation Enterprise

these assumptions are worked out to the point where an initial audit can be carried out. The assumptions are automatically created by the advice programme on the basis of statistical comparative values and discussed and, if necessary, modified by the advisors and entrepreneurs.

Once all plans for location, space, equipment, staff, costs and prices have been determined, the company can be established according to plan. Measures follow to establish the business. The loan with People's Bank covers the amount of all costs in the first year and includes a repayment plan for the next 10 years. The intranet and internet pages contain all the necessary information about the company and a sales function for online orders. All necessary insurances are taken out, company bank accounts are created at People's Bank and employees are trained in handling the programmes for digital administration. After about 4 weeks, the on-site support at the companies ends.

For the next 11 months, the entrepreneur can choose one of the advisors or is assigned an advisor who will supervise him during this time. During the first 12 months, the business figures are reviewed monthly. In case of negative developments or developments not according to plan, the advisor contacts the entrepreneur and, if necessary, affected employees. The entrepreneur can contact the advisor at any duty period. If the sympathy between the two is no longer right, each can ask for replacement or transfer up to 3 times. In case of complaints against entrepreneurs, advisors can turn to the responsible Ministry of Economy. In the case of complaints against the Company Auditing Agency, entrepreneurs turn to their responsible Ministry of Economy. Accordingly, a responsible Ministry of Economy resolves the complaints.

20.7.7.6.3 Market and operational analysis

Company figures such as turnover, profits, costs for machines, materials, labour, advertising, distribution, prices, production and sales figures are checked digitally. During the automatic check, a comparison is made with all companies that have similar values. All measures of these companies that led to profit increases in the past are listed. For this advisory service, the entire data set of the intranet is accessed. Access is exclusively via the consulting programme, to which only Company Auditing Agency business consultants have access. The advisory programme calculates the workload in time, money and personnel, a sustainable utilisation of all workplaces, the purchasing behaviour of all consumers, the sales behaviour of all competitors and the cheapest purchasing options. The cheapest purchasing prices are determined by searching all online retailers on the Internet and through the Company Auditing Agency's Purchasing Department or the Procurement Office. In a marketing plan, sales are simulated and a demand test is conducted. The demand test is based on the data of how many consumers have bought from which competitors at which place at what time and how much. The marketing plan contains standardised distribution options, such as retail shops, online trade, network marketing and others, which are simulated for the company's market situation in order to find the best distribution option.

20.7.7.6.4 Profit maximisation

If companies are seeking to maximise profits, they can seek advice. In the subsequent Company Auditing Agency audit, all auditors not only record the deficiencies, but also request suggestions for improvement from each auditor. Work orders can be issued to the responsible state institutes to develop improvements. The scope of services is granted to all companies in the Social Market Economy and is therefore described by the Ministry of Social Market Economy in voting with the Ministry of Labour.[245]

This is followed by a market analysis. Suitable trade secrets, innovations and industrial property rights can be found via the Innovation Database, the Success Model Directory and the Ideas Directory and offered to the company for sale. When making the offer, the advisors ensure that only anonymised data is passed on and that secrets are only disclosed with the agreement of the owners. If there is eligibility for funding from the Innovation Fund or the Research Cost Fund, this

245 Ministry of Social Market Economy - 17.2 Profit maximisation

offer will also be made.

As soon as the market analysis is available, it is explained to the management or in a company committee and all necessary decisions are made for the operational analysis. The farm analysis is entered by the extension programme in real time and digitally simulated for all given scenarios. With this information, advisors can work with the entrepreneurs to determine the quantities and prices that will maximise profits. If the company is run democratically, the determination is made at a company committee.

Maximum profit is achieved when the company is law-abiding, environmentally neutral and achieves more profit in the long run than before and maximum profits where prices are at the monopoly level. This is achieved in the price-sales function where, firstly, the price is so high that marginal revenue equals marginal cost and, secondly, where the sales volume is high enough to support all those willing to pay the price, the So-called Cournot point.

20.7.7.6.5 Innovation consulting

If own or third-party innovations are to be imported, which the innovation auditors endorse, the business consultants can accompany the companies in the implementation. The Innovation Agency's workers work together with the advisors. The advisory service includes the necessity check of every investment and every withdrawal from the Innovation Fund. It also includes further training measures for entrepreneurs and employees, which are carried out by teachers in the company or in the educational institutions of the Ministry of Education. The advisors have specific marketing plans for innovative goods and services based on past successful market launches. Demand can be narrowed down locally, nationally or globally. A reliable simulation of demand for new offerings can only be done within the national boundaries where the Company Auditing Agency audits and the Ministry of Digital Affairs pools all statistics to produce simulations. The advisors establish contact with innovation auditors who have already audited the successful commercialisation of similar innovations in order to develop similar methods or buy in success models.[246]

If innovations are lacking but would be necessary, research projects can be accompanied by the advisors. In order to be able to bundle as much research expenditure as possible from many companies, the Research Cost Fund is examined for similar pots. Should the company itself be able to conduct research to serve one of the pots, it can use this to generate income that fills its own pot quasi as a quid pro quo. The advisory programme automatically examines whether similar projects can be found in the Research Cost Fund or those through which the company can generate a return. The advisors examine all possibilities for cooperation in voting with the Ministry of Education and establish the necessary contacts. Depending on the costs involved, schools, colleges, universities and institutes can be involved in research work for companies.

20.7.7.6.5.1 Introduction of success models

The business consultants propose suitable success models from the Success Model Directory to the companies. Which success models are suitable for the company is automatically determined by the data of all auditors of the Company Auditing Agency. If the entrepreneurs agree to the introduction, the business consultants take over the fees for the success model and include the fee in their final invoice to the company. They advise the company on what measures need to be implemented and assist them in introducing them in order to obtain certification for this success model at the next audit. The economic auditors certify the company at the next audit and collect data for the success study.

246Ministry of Innovation - 9.11.1.1 Innovation Fund, 5.3.1 Research Cost Fund, 4 Innovation Agency, Ministry of Planned Economy - 10.6 Innovation Enterprise

20.7.7.6.5.2 Innovation launch[247]

If innovations from the Innovation Database or the Ideas Directory are suitable, this is automatically displayed to the business consultants in their advisory programme. For this purpose, all data of the entrepreneur are compared with the data of all innovations of participating companies. If entrepreneurs decide to introduce an innovation, the business consultants take over the first licence payment and charge the company for it in the final settlement. They accompany the entrepreneur in the successful introduction of an innovation by drawing on empirical values of innovation auditors from companies that have already introduced the respective innovation.

20.7.7.6.6 Insolvency proceedings

In the case of insolvency, the business consultants become active after the economic auditors have examined an insolvency delay.[248] Within 3 days after entrepreneurs report insolvency to the Ministry of Economy of their economic form, the business consultants visit the company. The insolvency consultation procedure is the same as the procedure for Social Market Economy companies.[249] All data from the past audit are compared with the current data.

The first advisory service is to recommend whether the company can continue to operate or should close down. The business consultants use the data from the tax and economic auditors to determine whether a company can continue to exist economically in the long term or whether it will generate more losses than profits and thus become unable to pay or deliver at some point. They use the data from the auditors for business, technology and innovation to determine whether the company is operating in the best possible way technically and as efficiently as possible economically. They check whether all deficiencies can be eliminated or whether the company

---

247 Ministry of Innovation - 9.7 Innovation Database, 8 Ideas Directory
248 Ministry of Justice - 8.1.4 Insolvency delay
249 Ministry of Social Market Economy - 10.2.1 Management Consultancy

must be abandoned. The audit results are presented to the entrepreneurs and employees at a company committee. If the business consultants still see possibilities to save the company from bankruptcy, they list all possibilities in the audit result. In addition to the apparent examination by the advisors, future prospects are queried by the Algoracle[250] . This takes into account all the possibilities of other companies affected by similar house claims in the same or similar market. All entries from the Ideas Directory, the Success Model Directory and the Innovation Database are automatically checked for their suitability and suitable opportunities are displayed. Through the consulting software, different scenarios can be played through and the possibilities applied in each case can be displayed.

The employees and entrepreneurs can vote on whether or not to close the company. If the business is to be closed, the economic auditors take over the task of the insolvency administrator. If the company is not to be closed, the entrepreneurs and employees must implement the requirements from the second advisory service. If money is needed for this, the entrepreneurs and employees must agree to raise the amount within a period determined by the advisors.

The second advisory service is to adapt the rescue options to the productive capacity of the staff, machinery and administration and to implement them together with all participants. The advisory services for profit maximisation and innovation can follow if the second advisory service has been successful.

20.8 Audit[251]

The auditors of the Company Auditing Agency always audit directly on site at the companies. If possible, all departments should attend a joint audit appointment in the case of announced audits. During the audit, the company's figures are collected, which provide information on the development of prices, wages, costs, turnover, number of goods or services and losses or profits. Occupational safety, satisfaction and

---

250 Ministry of Digital Affairs - 15.3 Algoracle
251 §188.4 Statistics: BV Art. 65

the ability to innovate are queried via a questionnaire that employees and entrepreneurs are asked to fill out. The questionnaires are designed by the Institute for Evaluation and adapted for each sector, if necessary also for individual companies. All data collected will be supplemented with the data set from the Labour Directory. In the questionnaires, respondents can choose to remain anonymous. It must not be possible to identify employees in the audit report who do not wish to do so. The audit by the innovation auditors and the advice of the business consultants, as well as the use of the Innovation Database, are not permitted for foreign companies.

20.8.1 Audit range

All audits consist of at least four areas. First, it is the questioning of the employees on how the working conditions are and whether they have suggestions for improvement or have contributed since the last audit. Secondly, the economic key figures are checked to find excessive costs and to test the solvency of a company. Thirdly, it checks whether a company complies with all the regulations of its economic form, or whether ministries and state enterprises abide by the laws that apply to them. Fourthly, it checks whether all taxes have been paid or whether ministries and state enterprises have properly transferred profits to the state treasury.

20.8.2 Audit intervals

The ministries and their state enterprises are audited annually, private companies every 2 years. At least 2 unannounced audits must be conducted in 4 years. In the case of unannounced audits, the departments can audit on a date of their own choosing and do not have to audit together on the same date.

20.8.3 Audit costs

The price of an audit depends on the economic form of the company, the scope of the audit and the personnel costs for the auditors. The costs are financed by fees or taxes in the various economic forms. In the Planned Economy, all audits and the advice are Tax-funded, but the majority of the auditors must recommend the advice.

20.8.3.1 Audit costs in the Free Market Economy

In the Free Market Economy, the examination fee for the compulsory examinations is 0.25% of the turnover of the previous 2 years, but at least 100 euros. This amount includes only the tax, health and legality audit. The scope of services for the tax audit consists of audits of annual financial statements, company valuations, purchase, sale, foundation, transformation or merger of companies or parts of companies. The scope of services of the health audit consists of audits of environmental pollution and occupational safety. The scope of services of the legality audit consists of audits of reorganisation and insolvency plans, over-indebtedness, insolvency, embezzlement, international accounting and fair competition.

The audits of the economic auditors, technical auditors and innovation auditors are subject to a fee. They may be mandatory for affected companies if ordered in the audit report of the above mandatory audits. Companies in the Free Market Economy can purchase any of the Company Auditing Agency's services on a voluntary basis. The amount of the fees is based on the cost-covering amount plus a 10% profit mark-up. The examination for stock exchange readiness will be charged with the first share issue. A percentage equal to the cost-covering price plus 10% profit mark-up is added to the issue price of shares issued in the first year of listing. The annual Exchange Commission fee is equal to the cost-covering amount plus 10% profit mark-up and is payable on the sale of shares and bonds.

20.8.3.2 Audit costs in the Social Market Economy

In the Social Market Economy, all audits are Tax-funded, except for the audit of the innovation auditors. However, the amount payable is only due when an innovation also generates profits. The amount can be spread over up to 10 profit years, regardless of whether employees or entrepreneurs developed the innovation. The business consultancy is chargeable and is settled at an increased rate, which increases by the cost-covering amount plus a 10% profit mark-up over the course of the coming year. The payment can be spread over up to 5 profit years.

20.8.3.3 Audit costs in the Barter Economy

In the Barter Economy, the auditors' working hours are compensated in working hours for the auditees. The auditees have to perform their working hours in services assigned by the town hall of their Barter Economy Zone. There is a fee for the advice. A deposit corresponding to the travel costs and the working hours on the first day of counselling must be paid before the counselling takes place. The costs incurred are listed in an estimate. The specified number must be paid before the second day of counselling. If services are not provided, a refund will be made. If more services are provided, an additional payment will be made.

20.8.4 Audit sheet

The audit forms for the different companies and sectors are prepared by the Institute for Evaluation and can be accessed via the auditor's audit programme. The audit form includes all the necessary company data specified by the Ministry of Labour. The Ministry of Labour bases its requirements on the auditing methods of the world's leading auditing firms and management consultancies, such as Ernst & Young or PriveWaterhouseCoopers. Digital data processing is done through enterprise software such as that produced by SAP or Oracle.

Companies offering goods and services must also have these products checked once by the technical auditors. As with new vehicles, which first receive their approval from the Technical Inspection Association (TÜV) before going into series production, goods and services must first be tested by the Company Auditing Agency before they can be placed on the market. The technical auditors of the Company Auditing Agency are responsible for this. Goods are tested for technical soundness and durability, services for thorough, punctual, speedy and professional execution.

20.8.5 Questionnaire

The questionnaire is sent to the employees and they are obliged to fill in the questions within 3 days. If employees are on holiday abroad or sick, the questionnaire must be completed on the first following working day. The questionnaire includes all data to improve the economic form, enterprise policy, organisation, equipment, operations and strategy of a company or to identify dissatisfaction. When satisfaction is asked, a tick can be placed next to the scale for "idea". As soon as the tick is set, a text field appears and a possibility to upload data. The idea can either be entered via the text field or uploaded as a file. Contents of files must be described in the text field.

For the special evaluation in the review for democratic enterprise policy, employees are asked the following questions:[252]
Have they ever participated in a feedback session?
Have they ever had an idea for the product or production process they work in?
If so, how did they deal with it - did they get money for it?
If not, have they been told how to behave in such a case and what they are entitled to?
Do they choose their superior?

252Pateman, Carole 1970: Participation and Democratic Theory. Cambridge University Press, Cambridge. Pateman, Carole 2012: Participatory Democracy Revisited. Perspectives on Politics, 10/1, pp.7-19, DOI 10.1017/S1537592711004877. Rothschild, Joyce 2000: Creating a just and democratic workplace: More engagement, less hierarchy. Contemporary Sociology, 29/1, pp.195-213.

Have you ever been a superior?

What options do they have to complain about their superiors or co-workers? Are they anonymous?

Do they have problems at work with: one or more superiors or colleagues

If so, have they tried to change anything?

If so, what happened?

Do they change positions in the company? How ? Who decides where they go? How often ?

What is their salary? (we ask this to find out the wage ratio in the company).

Did a superior promise them something and demand extra work or a different job in return?

If so, was the promise fulfilled?[253]

20.8.6 List of deficiencies

All results of the audits and questionnaires may reveal deficiencies that are listed in the audit report. Serious deficiencies must be corrected and newly audited before the certificate and badge are issued. Minor deficiencies must only be corrected by the next inspection. Certificate and badge will be issued immediately and will be accompanied by a deficiency notice. Companies receive a list of all deficiencies as well as proposals and deadlines on how and by when the deficiencies should be rectified. The Company Auditing Agency offers the service of correcting the deficiencies for the company at a charge and uses the department of business consultants for this purpose. For companies in the Social Market Economy and Planned Economy, this service is Tax-funded. All implementation costs arising from the advice are borne by the company.

If deficiencies could have criminal law consequences, the legality auditors examine the case. For this purpose, the company or employee is visited at home, if necessary undercover, evidence is collected and if the suspicion is confirmed, a complaint is

---

253 Ministry of Justice - 8.1.3.4 False promises

filed before the responsible court .[254][255]

20.8.6.1 Freedom from contradiction

The auditors' deficiencies must not contradict each other, consequently neither must the prescribed measures. The auditors must reconcile their voting results with each other before the clients receive the results. In the case of deficiencies to be remedied, rankings are made as to which deficiencies must be remedied first. The ranking must not contradict the constitution and must put the health of humans and nature first, followed by the surplus of revenues over costs.

20.8.7 Verifications

If the list of deficiencies was so extensive that it is not sufficient to check the changes at the next audit or if serious deficiencies have occurred, a re-inspection with costs must be carried out. If the defects have not been remedied by the time of the re-inspection, monetary fines will be imposed in minor cases. If serious deficiencies continue to exist that pose a danger to humans and nature, the company will be closed down.

20.8.8 Audit report

The audit report includes all data collected and is similar to the reports of rating agencies, corporate audit firms and management consulting firms in the free world economy. All involved departments of the Company Auditing Agency state their findings, assessments, expectations and proposals. Care must be taken to ensure that the wording is understandable for entrepreneurs and employees.

---

254 Ministry of Justice - 5.4 Courts
255 Ministry of Justice - 8.1.3 Corporate criminal law

20.8.9 Certification

Companies that have successfully passed their examination receive a certificate that is valid until the next examination. The certificate is published on the company's profile in the Labour Directory and provides customers and investors with information about the company's economic situation. When goods and services are tested, the test results, individual ratings and grades are published on the certificate.

As a summary, for example, the sentence "This business runs optimised, low-loss, environmentally sound and to the delight of the employees" can be written. In this example, the company has been optimised by the business consultants, classified by the tax auditors as having higher profits than losses but with few losses, classified by the health auditors as environmentally friendly because end products have to be disposed of by other service providers at a cost, and evaluated by the economic auditors in the questionnaires as a company with high employee satisfaction. All words that have such a clear meaning are defined in the glossary of the certificate. Other words that have an incremental form are colour-coded green for "low", yellow for "normal" and red for "high". Grades from 1 for "very good" to 6 for "insufficient", according to the school grading scale, can also be assigned for individual test criteria.

20.9 Success Model Directory

If companies develop strategies on how to deal with a situation better than all other companies, they can also register this strategy in the Success Model Directory. Before registration, the success model must first be checked by economic auditors for its chances of success. The regulations of the Ministry for Social Market Economy in the Success Model Programme apply.

The Company Auditing Agency markets workflows that increase efficiency and offers these workflows to companies that expel an inefficient audit in the area concerned.

The auditors of the Company Auditing Agency determine

which business strategies are most successful and create a profile in the Success Model Directory. Initially, only the Company Auditing Agency and the affected entrepreneur have access rights. Companies can market their success models, such as innovations. The company secrets are shared with other companies, but they themselves must also treat the success models as their own company secret. On the homepage of the profile, the success model is only described in such a way that its advantages and, if applicable, disadvantages are listed and for which companies or industries they are applicable.

The auditors of the Company Auditing Agency propose to companies for which there is a success model whether they want to use it and pay a fee for it.

Once the fee is paid, the full description of the success model becomes available to the licensee on the profile. For the placement of a licence, 10% of the licence fee is paid to the Company Auditing Agency and 50% of this is distributed as a bonus to all auditors who were involved in the placement. The Company Auditing Agency also offers to import success models into the companies willing to pay. In this case, business consultants from the Company Auditing Agency come to the company taking out the licence. The advisory team includes auditors who have already visited and audited the company that developed the success model. All the companies that apply the same success model are together in a model group to share their experiences and results.

20.10 Institute for Evaluation[256]

The scientists for the statistical research activities are requested from state colleges, universities and institutes and are trained or further trained if necessary. The Institute prepares the bills for metrology in cooperation with the Minister of Labour. Metrology establishes all standards that can measure things or conditions in any way. This includes, in particular, units of measurement. The procedures for measuring things and conditions are developed, tested, verified in operation and certified by the Institute in cooperation with the auditors and

256§252 Metrology: BV Art. 125

advisors of the Company Auditing Agency.

The Institute keeps all the statistics of the Ministries of Labour and Economic Affairs and forwards them to the Ministry of Digital Affairs for publication. This includes, among other things, the calculation of the Gross Domestic Product and the measurement of what share innovations have in it. Innovation auditors check how much additional profits a company generates through an innovation. With this measurement data, the Institute for Evaluation examines the share of technical progress in the Gross Domestic Product and the resulting increase in the standard of living.

The Institute for Evaluation develops examination forms, questionnaires and algorithms for the statistical collection of all business data inland. This includes the computer programmes for examination and advice that the auditors and advisors use on their People's Computers. The Institute is supported by staff from the Ministry of Digital Affairs. Auditors, entrepreneurs and staff are involved in the development of the sheets and software.

21 Pension

Pension means exit from daily physical gainful employment and entrance into retirement with a lot of free time until death. The prerequisite for this is that citizens have made provisions for their pension. Pensions as monthly cash benefits are offered by pension insurance companies and the People's Bank. The task of the Ministry of Labour is to centrally administer all pension payments during the course of a person's working life in various economic forms, ownership or employment relationships for the citizens in order to ensure simple and secure payment of all amounts. The Ministry of Labour takes over the coordination of the individual ministries of economy so that their pension concepts do not exclude each other to the extent that depositors of small amounts or short deposit periods go empty-handed, but receive back the deposited amounts with interest. All pension schemes, except the pension account, can be terminated at any time in order to invest the amounts saved for the pension in another pension scheme or to use them otherwise.

Regardless of the economic form in which senior citizens wish to spend their retirement, they receive all the income they are entitled to in their People's Bank pension account. Retirees can choose from retirement age whether they want a monthly payout or a direct payment of the full amount.

21.1 Pension models of the ministries

The Ministry of Finance maintains the pension account at the People's Bank[257] for every nationals from the moment of their birth. Unclaimed amounts flow into the generation account[258] and to survivors as family-related pension benefits. Citizens are not obliged to pay into a pension scheme. If citizens wish to take their own lives by suicide[259] , all paid-in and interest-bearing amounts can be distributed via the testament. The People's Bank pension account payments go entirely to the Generation Account or to the Ministry of Finance, depending on what the suicide decides.

The Ministry of Barter Economy does not offer its own pension model. Residents support and care for each other based on their own agreements. Pensioners receive all the benefits to which they are entitled. If the pension is high enough, another comfort level can be booked at the town hall.[260]

The Ministry of Planned Economy offers the unconditional pension model. All nationals are allowed to move into the retirement homes to live and work in the Social Village until they die.[261]

The Ministry of Social Market Economy offers compulsory insurance for pensions as a pension model. There are two contribution rates in the pension insurance, between which the entrepreneurs and employees of the Social Market Economy have to choose. In the low comfort class, there are supported Residential Communities for senior citizens. In the high comfort class, there are cruise ships for senior citizens on

257 Ministry of Finance - 11.5.6 Pension Account
258 Ministry of Finance - 11.5.7 Generation Account
259 Ministry of Family Affairs - 11.2 Suicide
260 Ministry of Barter Economy - 5 comfort levels
261 Ministry of Planned Economy - 6.1.2.5 Pension

permanent world tours.[262]

The Ministry of Free Market Economy does not offer its own pension scheme. Insurance companies in the Free Market Economy offer their own pension schemes to voluntary customers.

21.2 Retirement age

The ministries of health, labour and finance jointly determine the optimal retirement age and put it to a vote of the people. The retirement age is a minimum age at which pensions can be drawn. People who work longer and pay into the system receive more pension. Citizens can decide for themselves whether they want to receive their pension at the retirement age and continue to work, or whether they want to forego the payment and keep the amount invested at interest for as long as they work. It is also possible to work less and have only the interest earned on the pension amount paid out monthly.

22 Switching to the new system

The Ministry of Labour coordinates the establishment of the economic forms and the Company Auditing Agency. All social, pension and long-term care insurance conversions are initiated by the Ministry of Labour and implemented in voting with the affected Ministry of Economy.

22.1 Introduction of the economic forms

The four economic forms are introduced one after the other. At the beginning, there is only the free market economy as the currently applicable domestic economic form. Gradually, state services in the Free Market Economy are eliminated until the requirements of the ministry for Free Market Economy are met and all other economic forms have been introduced. Finally, taxes are reduced and the business tax is lowered to the level of the requirements. The tax surplus finances the establishment of the other economic forms.

262 Ministry of Social Market Economy - 17.5.4 Pension insurance

The Planned Economy is introduced as a second economic form, replacing the costly welfare state with its cash payments. Once the Social Villages are operational, the remaining social benefit enterprises move into the Social Villages. The Social Villages are built by the unemployed and financed by the social benefit funds and supported by the Ministry of Infrastructure with construction machinery and skilled labour. Initially, this task is still shared by the Ministry of Defence and the Ministry of Transport.[263]

The Social Market Economy is then built up by incorporating all the remaining laws of the welfare state, compulsory insurance, workers' rights and employers' obligations into the Social Market Economy's rulebook.[264] After that, companies in the existing Social Market Economy inland can voluntarily opt for the new rules of the Social Market Economy and re-register their company. Companies, citizens and municipalities can immediately set up cooperatives as transitional solutions and operate in a similar way to the Basque cooperative Mondragon.[265] The Mondragon Basque cooperative and its many sub-operations are to serve as a template to make structurally weak regions of the inland competitive in the short term. They are the prototype for the later corporations of the Social Market Economy and companies in the luxury supply work area of the Planned Economy. Like the citizens in Mondragon at the time, unemployed persons join forces with a business concept. The surrounding residents express their demand, provide the start-up capital and use it to found a bank. Anyone who wants to become an employee has to buy into the cooperative. He gets this money back as soon as he leaves the cooperative. Wages and material costs are paid from the turnover and 3.5% is invested in research every year. 10% of the profits go to parenting and social work, 45% provisions for the business, 45% for the workers.

Independent of the introduction of the other economic forms, the Barter Economy is introduced. Large contiguous areas of state forest are demarcated and a capital city is introduced on

263 Ministry of Planned Economy - 21 Switching to the new system
264 Ministry of Social Market Economy - 19 Switching to the new system
265 https://www.mondragon-corporation.com

the edge of the Barter Economy Zone in voting with the local population.

22.2 Introduction of the Employment Office

The existing Employment Offices are taken over by the Employment Office, which is responsible for the employment exchange. The Employment Office takes over its new responsibilities and starts building the Planned Economy through the unemployed. Once the Labour Directory is set up and the Social Villages are ready, placement in all economic forms begins.

22.3 Conversion of the pension system

The conversion of the pension system will take place depending on the budget situation. If the pensions have to be Tax-funded and the state would have to go into debt for this, the following path will be taken. All pensioners without children will no longer receive a pension from the pay-as-you-go system. All pensioners with only one child will receive 50% of their pension from the pay-as-you-go system. All pensioners with two or more children receive full pension payments from the pay-as-you-go system. Foreigners only receive domestic pensions if they have paid into the pension fund for at least 40 years and if at least two of their children are currently paying into the pension fund through work subject to social insurance. All foreigners to whom this does not apply do not receive a state pension.

If the budget situation permits, domestic pensioners receive more money and foreigners in pension receive their personally paid-in insurance amounts paid out monthly until they are exhausted.

Should the budget situation show sufficient savings, the money is invested profitably inland and the generated return is paid out to the pensioners.

22.4 Introduction of the Company Auditing Agency

The departments of the Company Auditing Agency are made up of different authorities and institutes, which are state or public agencies in the service of national or regional governments. The Tax Offices are transformed into locations of the Company Auditing Agency, and tax officials receive retraining on the Company Auditing Agency departments. The best tax auditors move to the tax auditors' department.

The technical auditors of the Company Auditing Agency are former engineers of the Technical Inspection Association (TÜV). The Company Auditing Agency is structured similarly to the TÜV. Personnel and scope of duties are similar to TÜV and its Audit Departments for different goods and services inland. Similar to TÜV ratings, marks and ratings are given for different categories and indicated as an overall mark on the product. In addition, the Office of Weights and Measures is incorporated into the department of technical auditors.

Technical auditors are employees from state agencies for research and testing in the fields of physics, technology and materials. Health auditors are staff from state agencies for occupational safety and health, environmental protection and environmental health.

22.5 Changeover of agriculture

Chairs for permaculture are introduced at all colleges with agricultural sciences. Subsidies are being shifted towards permaculture. To compensate for crop losses in the initial years of growing the new ecosystems, conventional agriculture will be allowed to continue. Once the permaculture areas reach the productivity of the conventionally farmed areas, all pesticides, fertilisers and medicines are banned.

22.6 Conversion of the old ministries

All departments and units that transfer to the Ministry of Labour are listed below. If only the department or sub-department is named, all its units are transferred. If individual units are named, only those units are transferred. All departments and units not named are dropped. Existing staff adapt their tasks to the new requirements. The corresponding names of the units can usually be found as keywords in the running text.

22.6.1 Federal Ministry of Labour and Social Affairs[266]

DA Digitalisation and the world of work

II Labour market policy
Unemployment insurance, Observation and analysis of the labour market, Labour market statistics, Financial issues of labour market policy
Active labour market promotion, career guidance, training placement, training promotion, education and employment system, promotion of vocational education and training, labour market issues of special groups of people, promotion of employment and self-employment.

III Labour law, occupational safety and health

IV Social security, old-age provision
Accident insurance, Pension insurance, Supplementary old-age provision, Benefit law, Miners' insurance, Old-age insurance, Financing pension insurance, Insured group of persons, Family-related pension benefits, Old-age insurance for farmers, Supplementary old-age provision Occupational pension scheme, Rehabilitation benefit law

V a Prevention, Rehabilitation and Disability Policy
Participation of severely disabled people, workshops for disabled people, assessment in the law on severely disabled people and in social compensation law, general and inter-agency law on the participation of people with disabilities, implementation of the United Nations Convention on the Rights of Persons with Disabilities, Focal Point, National Action Plan

266https://www.bmas.de/SharedDocs/Downloads/DE/Ministerium/ bmas-organigramm.pdf Status: 01.05.2019

22.6.2 Federal Ministry of the Interior, for Building and the Homeland[267]

D Public service
state service and Career Law, Federal Personnel Committee, Remuneration Law, Pension Law, Labour Law and Collective Bargaining Law, Allowance Law, Travel Law, Relocation Expenses Law, Occupational Safety and Health Law

22.6.3 Federal Ministry for Economic Affairs and Energy[268]

I Economic policy
Federal enterprises, central office for participation issues, public orders, Procurement Review Board

22.6.4 Federal Ministry of Justice and Consumer Protection[269]

II Criminal law
Commercial Central Register

III Trade and Commercial Law
Group law, restructuring law, accounting law, publicity, auditing law, commercial and company register, law of commercial transactions and commercial status, securities law, consumer policy in the field of financial services, financial market law
Consumer information law, agricultural and forestry law, cartel law and law against unfair competition, public procurement law

IV Constitutional and Administrative Law, International and

267https://www.bmi.bund.de/SharedDocs/downloads/DE/veroeffentlichungen/themen/ministerium/organigramm-bmi.html Status: 25.03.2019
268https://www.bmwi.de/Redaktion/DE/Downloads/M-O/organisationsplan-bmwi.pdf?__blob=publicationFile Version: 15.02.2019
269https://www.bmjv.de/SharedDocs/Downloads/DE/Ministerium/Organisationsplan/Organisationsplan_DE.pdf;jsessionid=A807B5B1F5EFC74825E8B2A6508405BE.2_cid297?__blob=publicationFile&v=131
Viewed on: 14/05/2019

European Law
state service law, labour and social law

V Consumer Policy, Digital Society, Consumer Enforcement
Strategy and fundamental issues of consumer policy, international consumer affairs, consumer law enforcement, consumer research, consumer education, sustainability, consumer policy in civil society, consumer organisations, coordination of project funding, research officer
Consumer information, consumer goods, product safety, special consumer groups

22.6.5 Bavarian State Ministry of Justice[270]

D Civil law and consumer law
Company law, civil law consumer protection, insolvency law

22.6.6 Federal Ministry of Finance[271]

VII B Financial market regulation

VIII C Infrastructure and contaminated site management
Fundamental issues of life-cycle oriented procurement

22.6.7 Federal Ministry of Food and Agriculture[272]

4 Agricultural markets, food industry, exports
Agricultural markets, food industry, animal products, plant products, common market organisation, food industry, quality policy
Competition law, land market, international commodity policy,

---

270https://www.justiz.bayern.de/media/pdf/orgplan/organigramm__18042019.pdf Status: 18.04.2019
271https://www.bundesfinanzministerium.de/Content/DE/Downloads/Ministerium/organigramm.pdf?__blob=publicationFile&v=27 Status: 01.05.2019
272https://www.bmel.de/SharedDocs/Downloads/DE/_Ministerium/Organisationsplan.pdf;jsessionid=273685EE44CB88915756D4E49ACE8F5D.live841?__blob=publicationFile&v=8 As of May 2019.

exports

5 Forest, sustainability, renewable raw materials
Forest, hunting and forestry policy municipal, national, international, sustainable forest management, timber market
Sustainability and climate protection, climate impacts

6 European Union Affairs, International Cooperation, Fisheries
Fisheries Structural and Market Policy, Marine Environmental Protection, Responsible Entity EMFF, Marine Fisheries Management and Control, IWC

7 Agricultural production, horticulture, agricultural policy
Agriculture, Crop production, Grassland, Organic farming, Animal and technology
Statistics, planning basics, knowledge management

8 Rural development, digital innovation
Green appeals, education, individual promotion, banks
Digital innovation

Contact form

Dear reader
If you would like to make what you have read come true, in whole or in part, together with other like-minded people, I offer you several possibilities with this contact form. Fill it out, tear out the page and send it by post to:
Andreas Seidl, P.O. Box 1206, 63488 Seligenstadt / Germany

Or send the details to:
Phone: 0049 1522 818 2243 (whatsapp, telegram, signal)
Email: andreas.seidl2022@web.de

Please mark with a cross:
O   I want to found a dynamic People's Party.
O   I want to donate money for implementation.
O   I want contacts with like-minded people in my area.

Forename: _____

Surname: _____

Please fill in only the contact option through which a reply should be made.

Street, house no.:   _____

Postcode, city, country: _____

Phone: _____

Email address: _____